fabric remix

fabric remix

REPURPOSE & REDECORATE
with Simple Sewing & Easy Upholstery

Sandy Stone

LARK
CRAFTS

A Division of Sterling Publishing Co., Inc.
New York / London

Senior Editor:
Valerie Van Arsdale Shrader

Assistant Editor:
Gavin R. Young

Art Director:
Megan Kirby

Illustrator:
Sandy Stone

Photographer:
Patrick Fox

Stylist:
Lisa Evidon

Cover Designer:
Megan Kirby

Supplemental Photography:
Sandy Stone

Library of Congress Cataloging-in-Publication Data

Stone, Sandy, 1958-
  Fabric remix : repurpose & redecorate with simple sewing & easy upholstery / Sandy Stone. -- 1st ed.
    p. cm.
  Includes index.
  ISBN 978-1-60059-485-4 (pb-pbk. with flaps : alk. paper)
  1. Upholstery. 2. House furnishings. I. Title.
  TT198.S895 2010
  684.1'2--dc22

                    2009052366

10 9 8 7 6 5 4 3 2 1

First Edition

Published by Lark Books, A Division of
Sterling Publishing Co., Inc.
387 Park Avenue South, New York, NY 10016

Text © 2010, Sandy Stone
Photography © 2010, Lark Books, a Division of Sterling Publishing Co., Inc.
Illustrations © 2010, Sandy Stone

Distributed in Canada by Sterling Publishing,
c/o Canadian Manda Group, 165 Dufferin Street
Toronto, Ontario, Canada M6K 3H6

Distributed in the United Kingdom by GMC Distribution Services,
Castle Place, 166 High Street, Lewes, East Sussex, England BN7 1XU

Distributed in Australia by Capricorn Link (Australia) Pty Ltd.,
P.O. Box 704, Windsor, NSW 2756 Australia

The written instructions, photographs, designs, patterns, and projects in this volume are intended for the personal use of the reader and may be reproduced for that purpose only. Any other use, especially commercial use, is forbidden under law without written permission of the copyright holder.

Every effort has been made to ensure that all the information in this book is accurate. However, due to differing conditions, tools, and individual skills, the publisher cannot be responsible for any injuries, losses, and other damages that may result from the use of the information in this book.

If you have questions or comments about this book, please contact:
Lark Books, 67 Broadway, Asheville, NC 28801
828-253-0467

Manufactured in China

ISBN 13: 978-1-60059-485-4

For information about custom editions, special sales, premium and corporate purchases, please contact Sterling Special Sales Department at 800-805-5489 or specialsales@sterlingpub.com.

For information about desk and examination copies available to college and university professors, requests must be submitted to academic@larkbooks.com. Our complete policy can be found at www.larkbooks.com.

This book was printed on recycled paper with agri-based inks ♻

For Mom, whose oft-repeated phrase "Why buy something when you can make it yourself for less!" still rings in my ears, and for Dad ("Do what your mother says!"). I miss you both.

contents

introduction

"So, what do you do?" This question, I'm embarrassed to say, causes me some anxiety. It may well be the reason I avoid large social gatherings with strangers. It cannot be answered with one simple statement like, "I do upholstery work," or "I recycle things." The layered nature of my craft requires a little more explanation and a few photographs to help people see the light. I upcycle, repurpose, sew, upholster, glue, staple, alter…in short, I use many different skills and techniques to create new objects from old.

Like many natural-born bargain hunters (a genetic trait—thanks, Mom), I've always been a chronic scavenger of thrift shops, estate sales, and garage sales. While shopping this way, I became increasingly drawn to the vintage clothing, furniture, and textiles one often comes across when searching through these venues. As my appreciation of vintage wares developed, so did the accumulation of salvaged treasures in our home. These materials began to find their way into my projects and eventually led to a game where I challenged myself to limit my use of new materials wherever possible. The game grew until I was tinkering with found furniture. This spurred my desire to learn upholstery and slipcover construction, which, in turn, rekindled my relationship with my sewing machine. That's when I became an artful recycler, incorporating virtually only used materials in my projects.

These raw materials themselves, then, are my true inspiration. When I head into the "field," there is almost never an agenda or specific item in my mind. It's all about the eyes—they lead me to the goods, and I bring them home. What happens after that is just three-dimensional doodling.

Maybe the best way to explain the process is to describe one of these incidents, so here's the "zipper tale" to help illustrate.

One morning while on a typical rescue mission (estate-sale shopping), my eyes fell on a large box with a few zippers hanging out of it. To my delight, I found that this box was absolutely stuffed with nothing but zippers! There were easily more than 100 of them—every length and color imaginable—some of them still wearing fragments of the garments they were torn from. And (here's the best part) they all had metal teeth! My favorite! It sounds silly, I know, but I honestly felt as though I'd uncovered the family jewels. Maybe it was the mass quantity that thrilled me, or the curious fact that someone had taken such great pains to save them. Most likely it was the price—about what you pay for a latte. They were all mine.

Once home, I dumped the zips onto my worktable and admired the glittering, snaky mound. As I fingered the thoughtfully styled pulls and markings, it occurred to me that this fine invention was hugely underappreciated. I now saw the metal zipper as a lovely work of design and engineering, not something to be hidden in the seam of a dress or at the back of a sofa cushion. These zippers deserved to be treated with more dignity.

My eyes really wanted to enjoy the colorful strips as a group, so my hands followed orders and began to sew the collection together. This process took hours and was completely mesmerizing. It grew into a heavy blanket about the size of an afghan. I threw it over an old coffee table waiting to be refinished, and suddenly I had a new piece of furniture. Not to mention, it was made of 100 percent recycled materials. Guilt-free decorating with personal style—that's my motivation.

My aim in *Fabric Remix* is to show you how exciting, easy, and liberating this process can be. You'll begin to see old things in a new light when you learn to ignore traditional methods of decorating—going against the grain is all part of the fun! In the following pages, you'll find ideas on alternative places to shop and ways to experiment with the types of goods you might find there. I've also included step-by-step instructions on how to repurpose various textiles (from petticoats to trampolines) in ways you may never have considered before. The lovely photography will not only jump-start your creative endeavors, but it will also demonstrate how to situate items in the home and present recycled furnishings with the distinctive look they deserve and command—a look that will function very well in your own home.

This book is full of projects conceived from a spirit of adventure that I hope will motivate you to look at the economic, ecological, and creative benefits of repurposing. But there's yet another bonus! Old things just seem to elicit curiosity. They've traveled through time collecting interesting stories to tell and have rich histories for us to imagine. When you combine all of these elements with your own personal touch, you will create a look that's intriguing to the eye *and* the mind, and you'll craft a home that feels warm and welcoming.

USING THIS BOOK...My unconventional work is presented in an unconventional way. I'll first introduce you to my sources of inspiration, places to hunt for amazing finds, and my favorite raw materials. Then I'll welcome you into my home, where you can view the projects from the book in the context of a real live house, where real live people really live. Next you'll get to see the projects up close and personal, and then you'll learn how to make them, with full instructions, how-to illustrations, and information on the tools and techniques I use.

gathering inspiration

What I love about poking around thrift shops or spending a morning hitting some estate sales is the anticipation of discovery.

The raw materials themselves are the basis for my work. When I feel the need for a little inspiration, my favorite sources are the used venues. By this I mean thrift stores, estate sales, occasional sales, and vintage shops. Since my blood type is "thrifty," it's the perfect mode of shopping for me. I simply don't have the disposable income to fund redecorating projects every few years (okay, months), and since my fickle nature requires that I change my slipcovers more often than some children change their socks, you will not find me in an expensive decorator shop. One could choose a fabulous new fabric from the affordable big box fabric store and decorate an entire living room around this fabric, but the minute that's done is the day the big box discount store buys the line and plasters the print over the surface of every object in the HOME section. When I shop scavenger-style I avoid these pitfalls and have the greatest potential for uncovering the most unusual raw materials.

I don't want my home to look like everyone else's. We all want to believe that we are unique in some manner and look for ways to set ourselves apart. Some people express themselves via their wardrobe, but "dressing" furnishings has become my chosen outlet for self-expression, perhaps because it's a little less personal and therefore not as risky. (I don't hesitate to put brightly colored giant flowers on a chair, but I'd never dare to don the same loud print myself.) Finding an odd, offbeat orphan chair that speaks out to me at the thrift shop and recovering it with a quirky drapery panel is more reflective of my personality than a chair I might find in a retail store.

Another reason to shop scavenger-style is the sheer entertainment it offers. What I love about poking around thrift shops or spending a morning hitting some estate sales is the anticipation of discovery. Granted, it takes patience and perseverance, but when you feel the thrill and gratification you get when you find that perfect prize and pounce on it faster than the next gal, you forget all about that hour you spent waiting in line in toe-numbing sub-zero temperatures or pouring rain. Occasionally I will come across the most exquisitely hand-crafted one-of-a-kind chair or garment or folk art piece and marvel at the care and time involved in its creation. As someone who works with her hands, I have an emotional response to these treasures and always feel the need to bring them home, almost like one would a stray puppy. (Sometimes I go home empty handed and then I feel like a stray puppy, but that's just the way it goes.)

Many of us have been shopping this way for years, all the while thinking we had some kind of sickness or were just cheapskates; turns out we're good eco-friendly people! Now we have the added benefit of feeling benevolent for extending the life of good old things and are helping to save the planet in the process. The green movement has increased our awareness of our buying habits, which is such a wonderful thing. My husband sometimes points out the irony of a perpetual rotation of goods among a small circle of us, but I think we all see it as a positive trend. It's old news that as a society we throw too much away, due in part possibly to the poor construction of goods. Buying vintage has brought my attention to this as I compare the solid, careful craftsmanship of former times to the shoddy mass production of recent decades. In my mind it is usually better to invest in designs that have stood the test of time, from both a creative and practical standpoint.

In addition to the economic, ecological, and creative benefits of decorating with used/vintage articles, there is also the intrigue of the stories they might tell us, since they've been around the block, so to speak. Transforming or altering a piece with your own personal flair adds further interest and incorporates your story into the mix (the remix, if you will). In my opinion, this is what makes a home warm, welcoming, and comfortable.

I feel there are absolutely no rules when it comes to decorating, and this is why I have learned to shop from every angle. Who says I must use upholstery fabric on furniture? No one's going to tell me I can't cut up an old dress and turn it into pillows. When you don't make huge financial investments in your materials, it gives you the freedom to experiment without intimidation. If you keep an open mind during your search and consider changing the roles of things, it can be very liberating. When out on the hunt my prey is basically anything that will pass through my sewing machine without breaking the needle. On the next few pages I'll discuss the places I frequent for scavenging; in The Raw Materials (page 16), I go into more detail about the wondrous items I work with.

Two hands aren't enough!
I love to hunt for bargains
to repurpose.

11

Estate Sales

These can be found listed in the classified section of your local newspaper (or online). Typically they start first thing in the morning, and often you will encounter a long line if you don't arrive in advance of the start time. There's a numbering system in my area, and the ambitious early birds are issued numbers that serve as "reservations," and later arrivals are required to queue up after those with numbers. Estate sales are run year-round but the majority of them seem to happen in the spring and fall. Once inside, you'll want to head to the bedrooms for linens, clothing and accessories, living areas for furniture, and the weird conversation pieces are usually buried in the attic or basement. But you really never know what you might find or where, so I search every nook and cranny. These sales are your best bet for finding the real bargains. In the rare event that you encounter the over-packed house (a "digger's sale"), you can really go hog wild. Do the smell test before purchasing furniture and textiles: Mold and mildew are almost impossible to eradicate, and things found in a smoker's home will have that telltale odor, so keep in mind that all sales are final. Don't forget to hit the garage where you might find things like awning fabric, canvas, and the like. Homes that were occupied by crafters and seamstresses are where I'm able to collect many notions (buckles, buttons, zippers, etc.), trims, and fabric remnants.

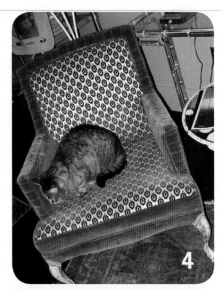

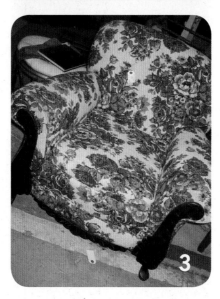

Anything and everything can be remixed and recycled. Keep an open mind when you shop. Here are some intriguing finds: **1** old quilts and textiles; **2** a funky lamp; **3** and **4** old chairs with lots of character; **5** barkcloth and various fabrics; **6** a perfect table.

A piece of furniture can provide a great canvas for upcycling. Look for things like this: **7** good bones; **8** interesting structure; **9** fun elements; **10** simple design; **11** unique styling; **12** classic form; **13** infinite possibility!

Thrift Shops

It's becoming increasingly harder to find bargains on vintage items in thrift shops anymore due to savvy processing managers. Still, some of my greatest discoveries have been seized in these places. For instance, a sleek mid-century cantilevered bent chrome chair for the price of a croissant? Can you beat that? In general, the goods that end up in thrift stores are gently used clothing and household items. I quickly scan the racks of clothing for unusual patterns and textures. It doesn't bother me anymore to harvest garments just for their fabric. After all, it's still putting things to good use. The home section is always full of pillows, which I give a quick squeeze to tease out the down or feather-filled forms. (I remove their covers to re-donate.) Polyester fiberfill pillows don't hold their shape and just aren't as comfy as feather, so I never use them. Some folks are a little squeamish about used pillows, but down pillows are actually machine-washable. You can throw them in the dryer with a tennis ball to fluff them. It may take a while, but they will dry eventually, or just let them air-dry on a warm summer day. Also check out the home section for draperies, blankets, bedspreads, towels, and other linens. You might also get lucky and find some handcrafted rugs, afghans, and quilts. Thrift shops are usually run by charitable organizations; you'll probably find a number of them in your area.

Though bargains don't necessarily abound in thrift shops, occasionally you get lucky: **14** a great mid-century chair and pillow; **15** a vintage fur; **16** used clothing and accessories; **17** a one-of-a-kind cushion; **18** unusual items, like shopping carts.

Vintage and Antique Stores

You're not going to find estate sale prices at these places, of course, but it's still a great alternative to buying new merchandise when you consider what you're getting for your money. If you appreciate quality craftsmanship, the old and unusual, vintage style, and eccentricities, you will find all of that at a good vintage shop, and the prices will be comparable to new pieces that lack these characteristics. Textiles are not usually found in abundance at these places, but I can always find a little something and be inspired by the other wares. Keep an eye out for seasonal sales and impatient dealers when they're ready to dump inventory that they're tired of moving around.

Occasional Sales

These sales are what one might describe as a step between estate sales and vintage shops. They are typically held one weekend per month, and the gist is to sell out each weekend so that each sale is fresh and new. They have similar wares as vintage stores, but because of a lower overhead they can offer lower prices. Occasional sales are usually listed in the variety or home and garden section of your local newspaper or, again, you can find them online.

When making my rounds I also include visits to fabric warehouses that carry close-out and deeply discounted yard goods. Situations arise where I have to break down and actually purchase new materials, and these provide the largest selection and the best value for your dollar.

Treasures can be found in all sorts of places. You never know when or where you might find: **19** awesome ties; **20** an antique birdcage; **21** cool wire filing baskets; **22** a most unusual lampshade; **23** genuine feed sacks.

the raw materials

"These pieces need to speak to my aesthetic in some way initially in order to get the creative ball rolling. The challenge here is recognizing hidden potential, and that just comes with experience."

What you put in your shopping basket is totally up to you, of course, but this is where I get to talk about some of the things that frequently get dropped into my basket (or crammed into the back of my van). My favorite recyclables are an ever-changing assortment, but repeatedly you will find me returning home with these signature items. You'll see many of these on display throughout the book.

Found Furniture

Most of the furniture pieces I bring home require attention since they're cheap, as-is purchases. Whether it's a big overstuffed chair or a small footstool, its form is the foundation of the project, and therefore the style and structure must be worthy of my effort. These pieces need to speak to my aesthetic in some way initially, in order to get the creative ball rolling.

The challenge here is recognizing hidden potential, and that just comes with experience. After many disappointing results, I've learned (I think) not to bother dragging something home simply because the price is right. I also gotta love it! Personally I am drawn to the clean lines of mid-century style, but for the sake of variety I like to stray now and then. Anything metal or on wheels makes me very happy.

Obis

The obi is part of traditional Japanese clothing, the sash worn around the middle on the outside of the kimono. Obis are no longer part of modern Japanese women's fashion and have become somewhat of a collector's item. The best of them can be quite valuable, but I continue to find them with very inexpensive price tags at a local thrift store that carries Japanese imports. The variety of colors, designs, and beautiful weaves are never-ending, and when taken out of context, these textiles lose their ethnicity and adapt to many different functions. You will find them in varying lengths, widths, and thicknesses, and they were also made from different types of fabric. What I love about them is that they are so long you can get a lot of mileage out of each one, and their edges are pre-finished, which is a real time-saver. Their stiffness offers structure to totes and purses, while their vibrant colors add visual impact. They're the perfect solution when you want to punctuate a sofa cushion or chair back. I like to be adventurous with jarring color and pattern combinations and make stripes by stitching a few together. The silk weaves are not as tough as some of the others, so I avoid using them in projects that need to stand up to wear and tear. Some obis are two layers sewn together with an

interfacing inside that makes them even sturdier, which can be helpful in some cases and not in others. For certain projects I separate the layers to reduce bulk. Trial and error will teach you when this might be necessary.

obis Part of traditional Japanese dress, obis were made of many fabrics, including silk, cotton, and rayon. They were worn at formal occasions, but were part of everyday attire, too.

Vintage Neckties

Neckties are ubiquitous, but I'm a little finicky about them so most just don't make the cut. (This could be said about everything I use, come to think of it.) The premium tie in my world is the handsome, geometric, narrow type of the 1950s. I often use them as purse straps. Since ties are normally constructed on the bias, the wider they are the more stretch they have. Narrow ties stretch the least, and most from that decade are made of a rayon/acetate blend as opposed to silk, therefore making a more durable handle. Some ties from that era are cut on-grain, which makes them easier to stitch together, creating "tapestries" that showcase their minimalist designs in a grouping. The "tapestries" can then be fashioned into bags and other items or used as upholstery. Real bowties (the ones that aren't pre-tied) also work well as handles, their unique feature being their adjustable length. The wild colorful patterns of the wider silk ties from the 1940s are also the kind I will grab. The loud, amusing designs make cheerful covered buttons or can add a subtle twist as cording around a pillow or cushion. The "tapestries" made from these ties are completely different in mood from those from the 1950s.

Used or Retired Clothing

It's easy to cut up stained or otherwise damaged clothing and textiles to reuse in my projects, but I've also given myself permission and artistic license to tear anything apart if I so well choose. Sometimes, and this happens more than I care to admit, I dismantle my own carefully crafted project to create the next one. Wool sport coats look very handsome applied to a wing-back chair. An A-line skirt is a nearly ready-made pillow cover. Fur collars can be stitched together to cover an ottoman. Need I go on? See how I used a vintage wool swing coat to make a cushion on page 54.

neckties Although they don't have the yardage that obis do, neckties are extremely versatile. Skinny ties from the 1950s make great handles or straps, while the dynamic prints popular in the 1940s provide visual punch and excitement to most any project.

Vintage Scarves

As bad habits go, vintage scarves are one of my real weaknesses. I'm too fashion-timid to wear them, but I like to look at them, which is the reason they cover the walls of my workroom. You can't fully appreciate a scarf's design while it's being worn, and I think they deserve full-frontal viewing, which is why I flatter them. The square and rectangular shapes and nicely finished edges scream pillow! And their translucent quality makes them the perfect candidate for lampshades and gauzy window treatments. A favorite activity of mine is "painting" with silk and chiffon scarves using decoupage medium (read about more about this technique on page 125). Apply one to a solid-colored vinyl chair seat or to the surface of a table, and you get an instant print. Layer scarves to create whimsical patterns on canvas, or sew scraps from badly damaged ones onto cardstock to make one-of-a-kind greeting cards. Scarves continue to suggest new uses to me.

scarves Just like neckties, scarves from the different eras reflect the personality of the times. You can find designs that range from prim and proper to mod and liberated!

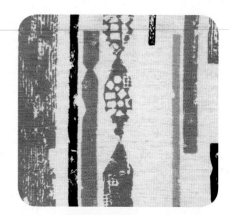

Drapery Panels/Barkcloth

You score big when you snap up some great drapes! The large amount of yardage allows for so many options. One panel can yield several pillows or serve as a coverlet or bed skirt, and may be enough to slipcover an entire chair. You might even want to use them as window coverings. Ha! Some of my favorite fabric found as drapery is the dramatic barkcloth from the 1940s, featuring large floral and leafy prints and then later, the cool geometrics of the 1950s. These textiles are becoming increasingly harder to find, and those in mint condition can sometimes be pricey. Silk fleur de lis, damask medallion prints, and brightly hued pop art prints from the 1960s are equally worthy. Be careful with draperies, though, as they are susceptible to sun damage. Several years hanging in a south- or west-facing window will lead to deterioration, so you need to do a strength test. Some old curtains have a rubberized coating on the backside that prevents this from happening, so they make good candidates for upholstery uses. Smaller projects are more suitable for the delicate examples.

barkcloth When I think of barkcloth, I get a picture of dramatic large-scale floral draperies that were often the backdrop of old Joan Crawford movies. At the height of its popularity in the 1940s, the designs were largely floral or tropical landscapes, but in the 1950s became more geometric and abstract.

The name comes from a primitive fabric that was actually made from the inner fibers of tree bark found in tropical and subtropical countries. The original barkcloth made its way to France in the 1920s, where manufacturers began to mimic its nubby texture using densely woven cotton fibers. When it arrived in the United States, barkcloth quickly became popular as a home decorating fabric. When I find real vintage barkcloth, it's almost always in the form of some kind of window treatment.

Miscellaneous Commercial/ Industrial-Use Textiles

Textiles that are printed with advertising graphics, company logos, and other text make unusual pillows and upholstery. Moneybags are one example; also, canvas signage, feed sacks, lumberyard aprons, and such. It's difficult to find these things in pristine condition due to the heavy use they've most likely weathered, but often they're fine after a good laundering, as long as you're not too fussy about a few stains or other minor damage. Many times these found items (especially signage) have grommets, straps, and metal hardware that are interesting to incorporate into projects as functioning parts or just as elements of surprise. Even heavily soiled materials of this sort can still be used; for instance, you can cut out individual letters to use for monogramming linens or totes, or for creating different words and messages to stitch onto T-shirts or other things.

Table and Bed Linens

Sometimes your own linen closet can be mined for treasures. When was the last time Grandma's fruit-print tablecloth saw the light of day? It might make a cute bedspread in a little girl's room. Or, maybe that old moth-eaten (but still beautiful) wool blanket would like to feel useful again. I once slipcovered a loveseat with a red striped blanket, which transformed it into a very cozy cabin piece. It's so fun to change the functions of things by rotating them through different areas of the house. Tired of the chair in your bedroom? Recover it with your bedspread and put it in the living room. Linen towels and napkins stitched together make a beautifully textured, updated version of the traditional quilt.

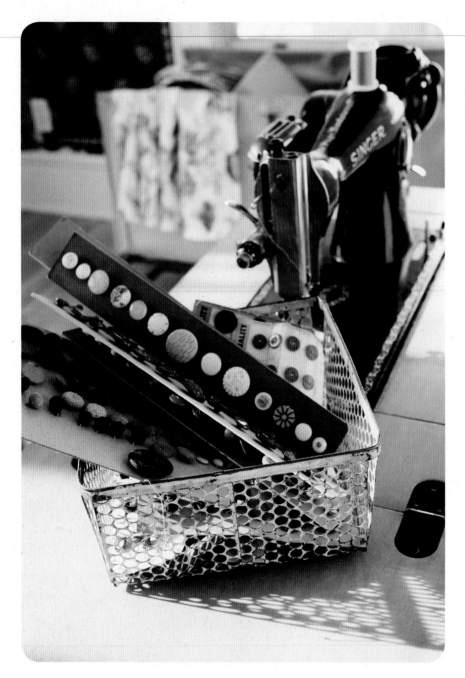

Accessories, Notions, and Trims

Belts can add a bit of whimsy to the ordinary. One of my most satisfying projects is a wood chair with a tattered caned seat that I repaired by weaving a new seat from salvaged belts. Belts make great tote handles also. Ball fringe and other types of trim are fun to keep around for embellishments and decorative edgings. Sifting through mounds of colorful buttons and buckles and zippers can entertain me for hours. Vintage cloth measuring tapes printed in black on a beautifully aged shade of ivory are a favorite collectible of mine. When a project calls for a special detail, I inevitably reach for these things.

notions Buttons, buckles, belts, and zippers are all yummy eye candy and perfect for embellishing all sorts of repurposing projects.

Paper Goods

I have a fondness for old yellowed paper, especially if it is written on in someone's lovely hand. Almost everything we see and read these days is typewritten, so I figure I should save a few handwritten examples to prove to my future grandchildren that there really were such things as pen and ink. Sewing on paper is a bit awkward but not at all difficult, and it's a novel way to add that "surprise" element, you know, the little twist that turns a good idea into a borderline genius idea!

When sewing on paper, set your machine to a wider stitch (about six per inch, which is a typical basting stitch) to prevent "cutting" through it. Backstitching will mess up paper, so I always cut the threads long enough to knot them. Several layers of paper can be stitched together if you use a heavy-duty needle (if you want to make a booklet, for example), but you'll have to experiment to find out just how much your machine can handle.

Care and Cleaning

If you're hoping that I'm going to divulge some great secret for removing stains or magically restoring damaged textiles here, I apologize. I pamper nothing! Most everything I use in my work must pass the standard washing-machine test, especially materials used for slipcovers and upholstery, as they have to withstand everyday use. (Even silk obis, which normally have a sturdy interfacing, can be washed on the delicate cycle in cold water and hung to dry.) There are exceptions, of course, namely neckties, which you should just spot clean, but I try not to buy soiled ones, so it's not really a problem for me; I'm also fairly adept at working around stains if I absolutely have to. Scarves

paper goods I often incorporate vintage patterns in my work, as well as other paper ephemera. Most paper items can be easily sewn in a standard sewing machine, with just a bit of practice.

should be hand washed in cold water, and line dried. Applying fabric protector to a finished project will protect it and minimize the need for frequent washing, which in itself causes fabric

to break down. Fabric for slipcovers should always be prewashed *before* construction, for the obvious reason of avoiding shrinkage when it finally needs to be laundered.

the remix at home

What disappoints me is when I overhear someone's reaction to distinctive furnishings as something they would absolutely love to have but can't imagine how to work into their home. This is complete and utter nonsense to me—what's stopping you? Sure, some of us are more interested than others when it comes to decorating, but I think we all want our homes to reflect our own spirit. We should love what we live with and look at every day of the year, and I'm living proof that this does not require deep pockets. If you're worried about people thinking you're a bit wacky, I urge you to dare to be different. Your friends will admire your courage and envy your distinctive flair.

The primary living area in my house is almost always a work in progress, for various reasons, but the biggest one it is that it suffers from "shoemaker's children" syndrome. My own house is always last on the to-do list, so a transformation can drag on for months and plans are always changing midstream, further prolonging the process. My house will never be "done" because I am never satisfied! But I'm always pretty sure that I'll get it right the next time.

What usually triggers the need for change is something like this: after weeks of complaining how tired I am of looking at a certain something, say a shabby cream-colored cabinet filled with cream-colored pottery and other cream-colored objects, the day finally arrives that I simply cannot tolerate it for one more minute. It's out the door...the whole shebang. Then there's the big empty space glaring at me, prodding me to find replacement parts. The funny thing is, the next great piece almost always appears immediately, as if it were just out there waiting for me to show up. Once the new piece is in, what occurs next, of course, is that old domino effect and, one-by-one, the other furnishings have to adapt to the new creature.

scarf-striped curtain
p 52

Entrance foyer

I love scarves but I feel so self-conscious when I wear them. I might as well carry a sign that says, "Yo, look over here! If you didn't notice, I'm wearing a very fashionable scarf around my neck!" Same with hats. Pillows wear scarves with such aplomb. They're the same shape, sometimes the same size...just a match made in heaven.

Scarves are really better served open to view and even prettier hanging in a window with light filtering through, a good reason to pull a few of my favorites out of a very crowded basket and stitch them into some curtains. I am not always happy. These curtains and pillows are always happy, and they do a bang-up job greeting guests in the entrance foyer.

In the living space

Can you believe that the couch in my living room cost less than a lunch? Of course, I had to shell out about four times that amount for the heavyweight linen (incredibly cheap warehouse purchase) that I used to reupholster it, but because I did the work myself I saved yet another bundle of cash. The bolster, once my winter coat, looks much better on the couch than it ever did on me, and I still get to admire its beautiful tweed pattern. The buttons on both the couch and the bolster are covered with silk remnants from the tie chair project on page 77, also in the room, to help tie them together visually. The mid-century bent chrome chair is the one I bought so cheaply, which was less than the cost of each one of those double-wide ties featured on the back.

Zippers are my jewelry. (Hmm, that just gave me an idea.) This zipper tapestry glitters in the sunlight that pours in from the clerestory windows. My kids and their friends used to play with it when they were younger… unzipping, zipping, unzipping…it's interactive art! Everybody loves this thing.

The giant flower chair originally had big, clunky square-shaped wooden arms, and I couldn't decide if they were stupid/good or stupid/bad. (I know, I know, more technical terms.) I had to remove them to make the slipcover anyway, and to be honest, I was probably just too lazy to put them back on. Many difficult decisions are made in this manner….

wool coat bolster
p 54

giant flowers slipcover
p 67

studio couch
p 61

zipper tapestry
p 71

IN THE LIVING SPACE...My cell phone rings. It's Kristi (good friend and owner of hunt & gather—the best vintage shop in town, or the country for that matter, where I sell my wares). "Get over to the sale at (such and such a place). There's a little couch in the basement that you're going to want and it's so cheap! See ya later, bye." Being the nice person that she is, she likes to hook me up with potential projects, for which I am very grateful, and often sends me hither and yon. It's usually worth the trip.

mid-century tie chair
p 77

In the nook

A friend of mine found these 5"x7" numbered canvas patches while shopping online. If you've ever watched a marathon or other type of organized race, you've seen that each entrant must wear a number on his or her chest. Well, that's what these numbers are, but a bit more special because they are vintage and left over from a long-ago bike race in France. When I saw them I told this friend that I thought it would be fun to work them into pillows or something. She tossed them into my lap and said "Well, go make me some of those pillows and you can have 'em all!" I stitched a bunch of them together to create the boxing for this cushion while I should have been making her pillows.

trampoline window treatment
p 73

window bench cushion
p 48

A NOOK...My love of typography may be a lingering effect of having spent some years working in the graphic design industry. For whatever reason, I'm fond of randomly incorporating graphic elements and printed materials into upholstery projects, such as this bench cushion. I also get a kick out of using something hard-edged or industrial where you would normally see something soft or dainty, e.g., this trampoline window treatment.

vintage scarf pillow
p 65

vinyl revival
p 75

IN THE SITTING ROOM...Vinyl upholstery has a distinctively mid-century look and it's a very practical material, but let's face it, it doesn't provide a very comfy seat. Applying fabric to just a portion of this sectional added a little softness to the surface, as well as some visual texture. It also helps to keep the sitter in place!

doggie bed
p 66

In the dining room

The obi placemats on the dining room table took very little time and skill to make, but look dressy and very upscale (which I am not), belying the fact that the material cost for each could buy you a cup of coffee. Very clever (which I am), and they are machine washable so I'm not afraid to use them. All it took to make the table runners was the energy to throw two obis across the table. The lanterns, originally outdoor fixtures, were another extremely low-tech alteration using scarf remnants. You can skip the electrician and opt for votive candles.

Our main floor is a drapery-free zone because we love our windows, but now and then privacy is a good thing. In this situation, one could buy a ready-made, flimsy, ho-hum folding screen and be done with it, or, make a pow(!) piece with your very own hands. This vivid privacy screen is merely chiffon fabric attached to a lightweight metal clothes rack, light as a feather and easily movable. It was so easy I made two of them, the second one using some beautifully aged handwritten journal pages.

embellished lanterns
p 45

obi placemats
p 68

mod garment rack screen
p 47

IN THE DINING ROOM...The obi placemats and table runner look sophisticated, yet were extraordinarily inexpensive and easy to make. You can quickly change the personality of any room by simply exchanging accessories.

In the kitchen

In my opinion a kitchen calls for no nonsense, and items with no function are simply not allowed. These chair seats, for example, are covered with a salvaged canvas sign onto which the lettering was applied with paint. I figure if it survived all kinds of weather during its advertising days, it could survive a few more in my kitchen without much trouble. The chairs themselves are made of iron so that makes the whole package close to, if not completely, indestructible. What I'm going to say next may surprise you, but it's true. If you can wrap a present, you can upholster a simple chair seat like these. It is exactly the same thing except you use fabric and staples instead of paper and tape. I'm serious.

I enjoy a good theme, just like anyone else, and since the chairs flaunt lettering, I thought it would be fun to carry the typography thing to the linens. Because, just like all of you, I have so much time on my hands, I like to fill it by cutting letters out of printed textiles such as feed sacks and lumberyard aprons and then play kitchen word games with myself. After I'm satisfied with my word finds, I stitch them onto linen toweling to entertain my guests. There are just too many hours in the day!

scrappy table linens
p 55

embellished wire basket
p 63

graphic chair seats
p 50

IN THE KITCHEN...The large letters on these chair seats give each one a slightly different look and are a fun surprise in the kitchen. The durable canvas signage they're made from make them almost impossible to damage. The silly word play on the linen towels continues the typographic theme.

recycled zipper pouches
p 72

sanctuary chair
p 46

In the bathroom

I love the fact that this chair spent the majority of its life in a church and is now wearing a towel in a bathroom, getting a slightly different view of things. I'm referring to the fact that it's not a big change from velvet to terry cloth, mind you.

The cute little wool cosmetic pouches have a similar background. They were made from… holey (sorry) blankets.

In the guest bedroom

Well, this is a somewhat sad story. It's the beginning of the empty nest, you see. Eldest daughter graduates from college, lands a fancy-pants job in the Big Apple, moves away, and leaves a big space behind. That is a void only a decorating project can fill—I know, maybe said daughter's bedroom should become a fancy guest room! I feel better already.

The old damask draperies adapted easily as a group to their new function as a bedspread and pillow sham, plus they shimmer (first time I've used that adjective when referring to my house). The flouncy (another first-time adjective!), lacy slips I used to create the bed skirt add a feminine frill (I'm running with this!) without looking like female undergarments (first time I've used that noun when referring to my house).

IN THE BATHROOM…When bath time is over a terry cloth seat is the perfect spot for a wee one's wet bottom. The pouches made from scraps make cute and practical make-up or travel bags and cost me virtually nothing.

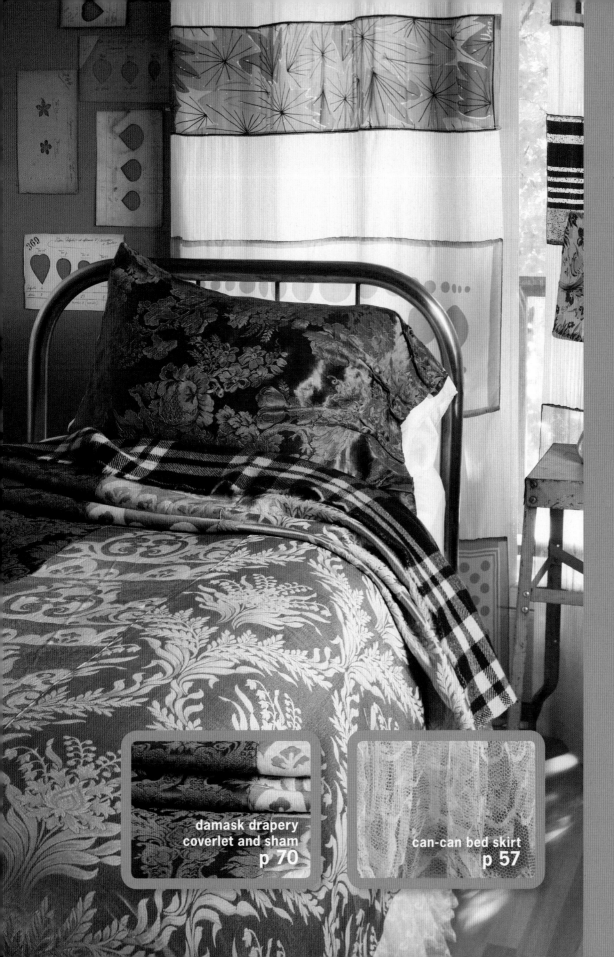

IN THE BEDROOM...The old damask draperies morphed beautifully into a bedspread to give the room a new shimmering look. The slips add a feminine touch without being too girly.

damask drapery coverlet and sham
p 70

can-can bed skirt
p 57

In the master bedroom

Under the padded linen and buckles of this bed lies an open metalwork headboard (hard and uninteresting). It's a much cozier place to be now after the simple addition of some foam and fabric. The tight linen slipcover is basically just an envelope to hold everything, and the buckles batten it down. Buttons are what one would normally use in this situation and I have plenty of them on hand (five carafes to be exact), but I really wanted metal buttons and they came up short. However, I did have several large metal buckles, which seemed like a reasonable substitution.

Money bags make great pillows and are so easy to make! Just cut them open, dump out the cash, and replace with feathers. (Well, that's not entirely correct since I've never found one full of dough.) I bailed the typewriter table out of a garage for practically nothing. To add some romance to all these utilitarian objects, how about a little mink, perhaps? Maybe a throw created from some dilapidated fur coats that were so beyond repair the only thing left to do was to upcycle their usable sections into something luxurious? Now *that's* romantic.

resurfaced table
p 76

buckled-up headboards
p 74

mink throw
p 53

RETURN TO
CENTRAL NATIONAL BAI
AND TRUST CO.

moneybag pillows
p 60

DES MOINES, IOWA

IN THE MASTER BEDROOM...The buckles on the headboard are a completely unexpected and lighthearted look, as are the moneybag pillows. But the patchwork mink throw wants to stir up a little romance.

In the studio

Trust me, this room is rarely this clean, and I feel a little bit guilty about the misrepresentation. When I'm in the middle of a project it's generally knee-deep with materials (occasionally hazardous), and every bin, basket, and cabinet is mysteriously empty. A very large shelving unit (not shown) that houses said bins helps me feel organized for short periods of time, but whatever I'm looking for is always at the bottom of the very last bin I rifle through! Keeping large quantities of raw materials close at hand is the key to the creative process, but I might need to rethink the bin method.

scarf-painted cabinet
p 69

IN THE STUDIO...Lots of seriously fun work happens inside these four walls, and ON these four walls, for that matter. There's a mathematical reason for the unconventional "paint" job (which was a precursor to the scarf-painted cabinet project)—stark white walls + staple gun + large collection of scarves x a wild hair = 1 project for Sandy. No surface is safe around me.

In the garden

After suffering through our difficult winters each year, we Minnesotans get the most out of our short but gorgeous summers by virtually living outdoors three (well, okay, two) months out of the year. Why not bring some style with us as we head out to the backyard? This sling chair was a cinch to make using two obis, and I managed to eke out a tote bag from the leftovers! The removable and washable orange pillow cover was fashioned from a gently used towel, making it very sunbather-friendly.

Yes, I know the bright colors will fade in the hot sun, but that gives me a great excuse to replace the fabric with something new next spring. In garden-speak, my furnishings (indoor and out) are more annual than they are perennial.

obi totes
p 58

obi sling chair
p 64

42

vintage bike seat
p 59

IN THE GARDEN...Another embellished basket finds an outdoor use as well.
And vintage fabric can elevate the most utilitarian of objects—a bike seat, for
instance—to a whole new level. I'm sure you can't help but notice that an obi tote
or two insist on going along for the ride.

project gallery

My motive in the art of recycling furnishings is ultimately to have some design fun on the cheap, while treading lightly on the earth. Instructions for all these projects are in the Make It section that begins on page 80.

I realize that many of the materials used in the following projects are not readily available to all, but my intent is to throw some light on the things that are often overlooked. We are surrounded by goods that may appear to be tired, but, with a little twist, can be made to look fresh again. Remember, there's no need to be intimidated, just a desire to express your true self in your home. Combining used goods is an endless source of entertainment for me and, hopefully, the results will amuse and inspire the artful recycler in you.

EMBELLISHED LANTERNS

PAGE 45

If I remember correctly, these decorative scrolled lanterns were found in a garage sale for, oh, next to nothing. After they had been hanging for a couple of months in the antique store where I work, apparently unnoticed, I decided I might as well take them home and have a little fun with them. The textured gold glass didn't thrill me that much, so I covered it with some translucent scarf scraps. The fabric prints add interest while still allowing light to filter through.

(make it on page 82)

SANCTUARY CHAIR

An antique carved wooden church seat enjoys an afterlife in a different kind of sanctuary. The irreverent treatment of a gently used, sculptured terry towel takes the serious edge off of this chair while making an inviting (absorbent!) spot to relax after a hot bath. Amen.

(make it on page 82)

MOD GARMENT RACK SCREEN

This fabric reminds me of *Laugh-In*, the TV show from the 1960s. I found many yards of it at an estate sale and couldn't resist; after all, it is Italian chiffon. Originally, no doubt, it was carefully chosen with a sexy, swingy mini-dress in mind, but sadly— for whatever reason—this mod print spent 35 years in a box.

(make it on page 84)

WINDOW BENCH CUSHION

PAGE 48

Once you've mastered the construction of a basic cushion with cording, you'll be well equipped to tackle many upholstery projects. The bold graphic numbers from these vintage racer's bibs add punch to this otherwise ordinary window bench.

(make it on page 85)

SCARF LAMPSHADE

Here's one more great use (out of 101 such great uses) for a pretty vintage scarf. It's easy to make, and just think how adorable it will look on (you know who) at your next New Year's Eve party.

(make it on page 88)

GRAPHIC
CHAIR SEATS

The large lettering on this canvas sign becomes just abstract shapes when randomly applied to the seats of cast metal chairs.

(make it on page 89)

BALL FRINGE FOOTSTOOL SLIPCOVER

PAGE 51 A simple slipcover is a wonderful quick fix for a tattered piece of furniture. Adding three miles of ball fringe makes it not-so-quick, of course, but the result is a very girly conversation piece.

(make it on page 90)

SCARF-STRIPED CURTAIN

Simple tab-top curtains are plentiful at thrift shops, and you can leave the store feeling very smug when you find a pair for the price of a sandwich. Of course, when you get them home you may discover that they're way too short because you are not organized and did not have the window measurements with you when you went shopping. Not to worry; there's almost always a lovely way to fix a mistake, such as adding a scarf or two.

(make it on page 91)

MINK THROW

Yes, we are broaching a touchy subject here. But political implications aside, what is a person to do when she is gifted with two or three unwearable vintage fur coats?

(make it on page 92)

WOOL COAT BOLSTER

PAGE 54 This bolster was fashioned from a gorgeous three-quarter-length vintage wool swing coat that I scored at a thrift shop. It was the warmest, classiest coat I'd ever owned, but it was a bit out of proportion to my petite frame. Despite that, I just couldn't bring myself to give it away!

(make it on page 93)

SCRAPPY TABLE LINENS

Most of my "bread and butter" work consists of custom slipcovers, and many of them are made of linen, which is almost always my "go-to" fabric. It's one of the very few fabrics I actually seek out to purchase new, because I love its hand, drape, texture, and washability. Every little leftover scrap of linen is worth saving, in my opinion. Here's one fun way to utilize them while incorporating a challenging game of Boggle into the mix.

(make it on page 93)

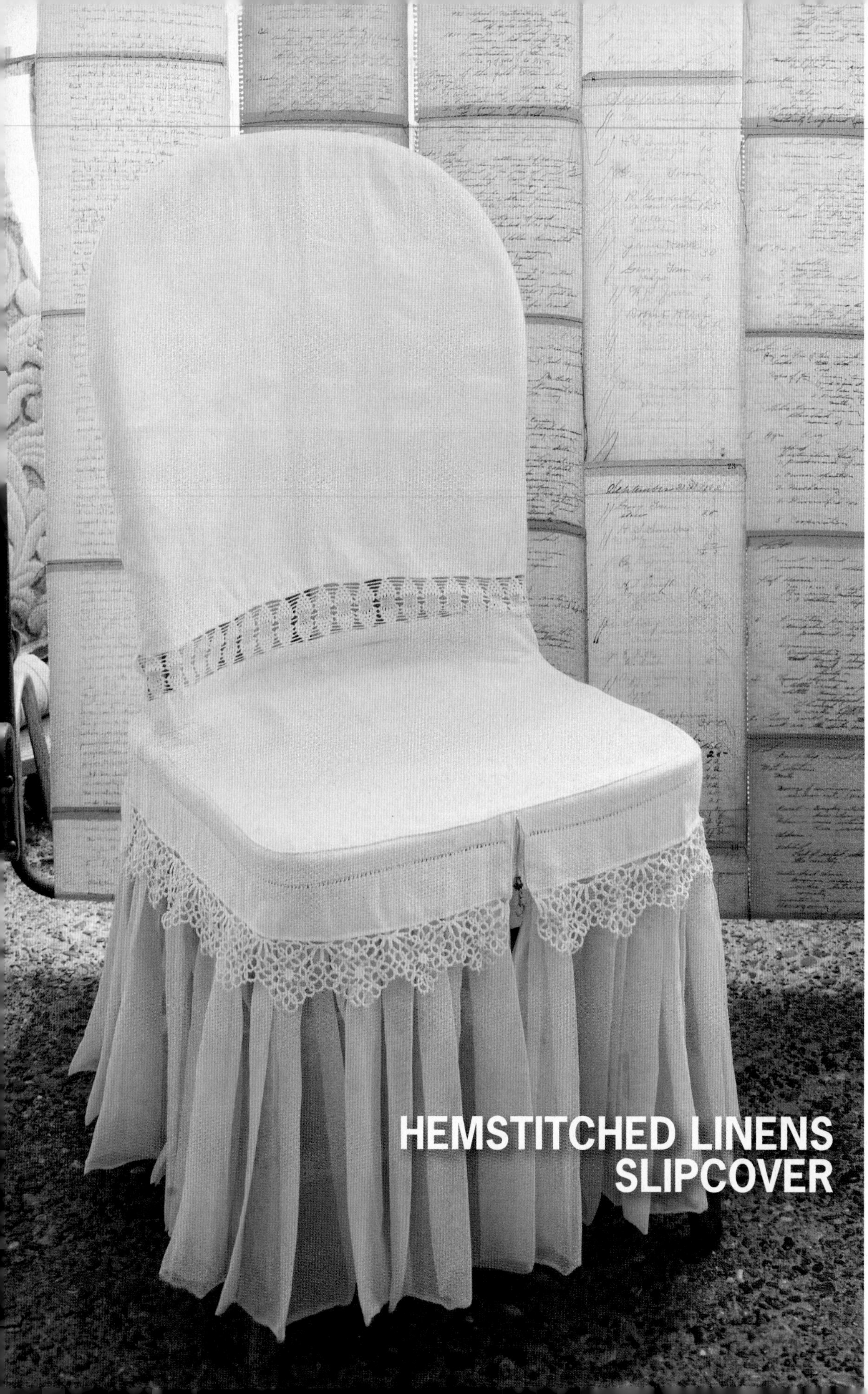

HEMSTITCHED LINENS SLIPCOVER

PAGE 56

Serendipity often steers the creative process. While I was digging through one of my remnant bins, looking for inspiration for this chair project, I came across two lovely vintage linen towels with delicate handwork. (Where did these come from?) I was so delighted by the way they fit the chair, and that they combined in such a way that made so little waste—apparently it was meant to be.

(make it on page 94)

CAN-CAN BED SKIRT

PAGE 57

When my girls were little, they loved to play dress-up with old crinolines and flouncy petticoats; I grew up calling them *can-cans*. The girls would twirl like flamenco dancers until they fell down dizzy. Vintage slips with layered ruffles are ready to skirt anything, with a few easy adjustments. They can be found in a vast array of colors if you want to make a bolder statement.

(make it on page 95)

OBI TOTES

If you've ever tried on a vintage dress, then you know how tiny (or well-girdled) women's waists were at one time. I've got the dress belts to prove it. Believe me, they're never going to make it around my middle, but they make charming tote handles, so I keep collecting them. Vintage bowties also work! I offer you a couple of variations.

(make it on page 96)

**VINTAGE
BIKE SEAT**

A photo stylist and I were having a conversation in my backyard when she noticed (stylists notice everything, you know) the ragged seat on my daughter's bike as it leaned against a tree. She said, "Wouldn't it be cute if you made a fabric cover for that old seat?" I wish I'd thought of that!

(make it on page 97)

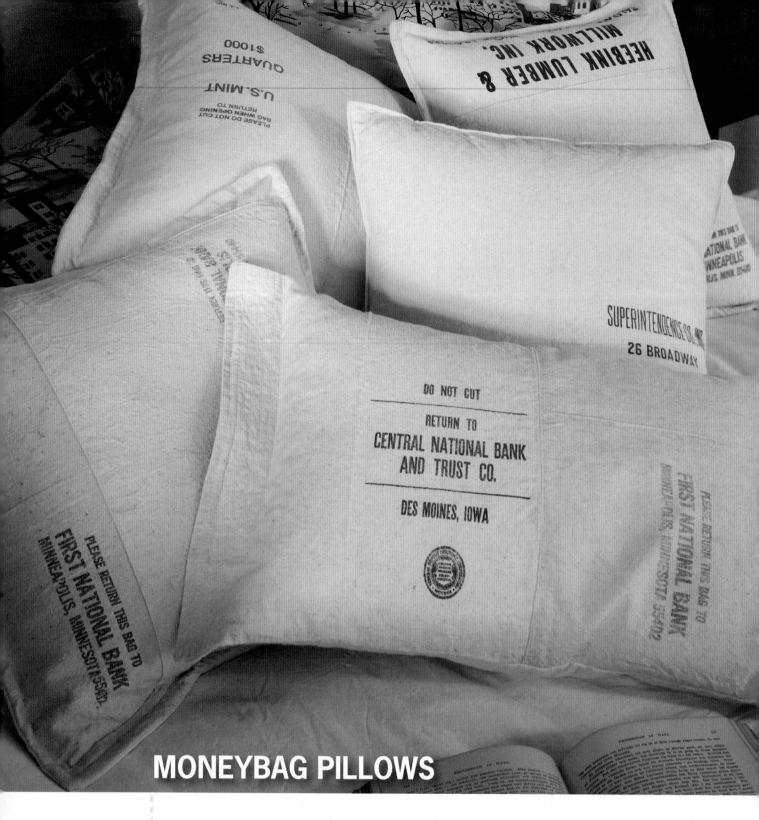

DO NOT CUT

RETURN TO
CENTRAL NATIONAL BANK
AND TRUST CO.

DES MOINES, IOWA

MONEYBAG PILLOWS

PAGE 60   Used cotton canvas is one of my favorite materials to work with. When I found a basket full of moneybags and lumberyard aprons at an occasional sale, I knew I had to have all of them. I didn't know why at the time, but they later turned into some very soft and cozy pillows.

(make it on page 98)

STUDIO COUCH

PAGE 61

A couch like this may look like a daunting project, but if you'll notice, it's basically made from three separate cushions. When you break it down and approach it cushion by cushion, it's really not that scary.

(make it on page 99)

CANVAS SIGNAGE SATCHEL

PAGE 62

I realize that hand-painted canvas signage does not come into one's possession on a regular basis. Since I have friends in the scavenging business, and friends who just like to contribute to the insanity, strange things sometimes land on my doorstep. That said, this project illustrates how any sturdy material can be constructed into a handy carryall, be it your worn-out boat cover, sail, or even an old paint-splattered drop cloth.

(make it on page 100)

**EMBELLISHED
WIRE BASKET**

This is a perfect beginner's project, with basic basket weaving so easy you could do it blindfolded (well, almost). Start with an ordinary wire locker or bicycle basket—the more bent and twisted the better—and make it extraordinary with interesting, uncommon embellishments.

(make it on page 101)

OBI SLING CHAIR

Obis are among the prettiest and most versatile textiles I have encountered over the years. They can be found in a variety of widths, colors, and beautiful brocades, as well as other weaves. Most of us don't need them to cinch our kimonos, but they have a lot of potential in other areas. For example, they were the perfect remedy for this ailing deck chair.

(make it on page 102)

VINTAGE SCARF PILLOW

PAGE 65 A scarf worn as intended is a very lovely thing, especially for us women of a certain age. But now and then a fabulous design deserves to be opened up to full view, to receive our complete appreciation. Transformed into pillows, vintage scarves are a treat not only for the eyes, but also for a weary head.

(make it on page 102)

DOGGIE BED

PAGE 66

Teach an old rug new tricks! Handcrafted rugs like these were a popular craft during an era when our mothers had that love affair with polyester double knit. The ruffled circular design is not only attractive, but also a visual aid for your pooch as he twirls to arrange himself properly! The poly washes up so nice, too.

(make it on page 104)

GIANT FLOWERS SLIPCOVER

A simple chair like this one is the perfect candidate for a first-time slipcover endeavor. If you don't have much invested in materials (recycled bedspread, perhaps?), there's really no reason to be intimidated. This cheerful cotton slipcover, formerly a daybed cover, instantly perked up this lifeless old chair. Four easy pieces. Sixty minutes. Done.

(make it on page 105)

OBI PLACEMATS

PAGE 68 Yes, I know, not everyone has a local source for inexpensive obis. For some of you, the hardest part of this project will be locating them. But if and when you do, I guarantee you will be inspired, and the rest will be easy. Here is yet another way to create something beautiful and useful with obis.

(make it on page 106)

SCARF-PAINTED CABINET

Decoupage is such a great medium for surface design. One day while experimenting with it, I pulled out a vintage polka-dot chiffon scarf and discovered that it accepted the g ue really well. The result was an almost instant hand-painted look without all the time, tedium, or expertise. Become a "painter" yourself with this method, and totally impress your family and friends.

(make it on page 107)

DAMASK DRAPERY
COVERLET AND SHAM

If Scarlett O'Hara can get away with wearing curtains, I don't see why I can't use them as a bedspread. Mixing different patterns makes this project much more interesting than her dress was. As far as the sham goes, the pleats on this drapery panel looked so pretty to me that it seemed a shame to trim them off. One should, however, remove the hooks!

(make it on page 108)

ZIPPER TAPESTRY

PAGE **71**

This piece was inspired by an anonymous (genius) collector of giant metal zippers, whose stash found its way into my possession. I discovered a new form of meditation while sewing them together into this tapestry. Finding this many metal zippers will be the more difficult challenge.

(make it on page 109)

RECYCLED ZIPPER POUCHES

You already know about my zipper fetish. These zippers are just as I found them, with the fabric from their previous homes still attached. The raw, hairy edges are so fun—showcase items, in my opinion! The old wool blanket pieces serve as a nice backdrop, don't you think? The smallest pouch is made from a section of an obi.

(make it on page 110)

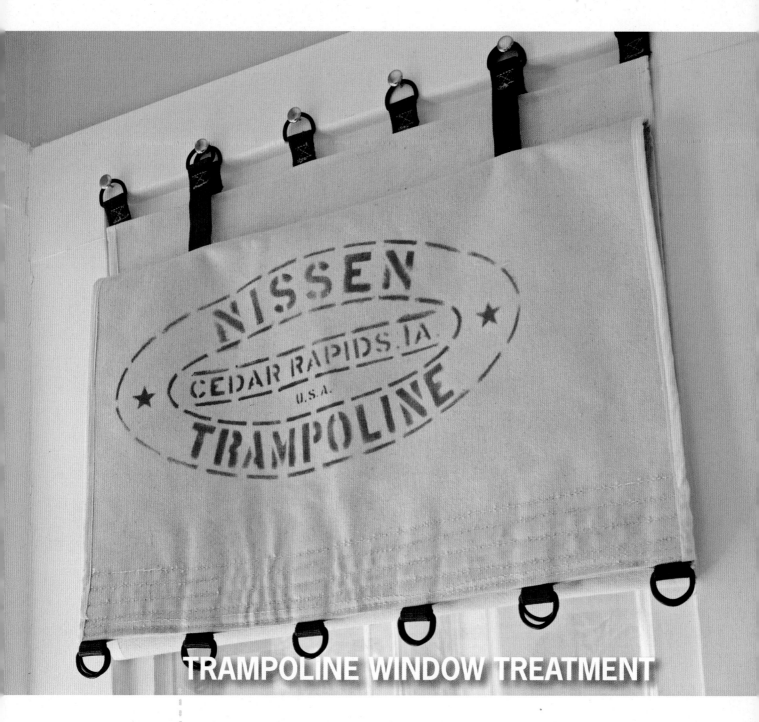

TRAMPOLINE WINDOW TREATMENT

PAGE 73

Have you been wondering what to do with that trampoline in the backyard, now that the kids are all grown up? Bet you never thought of this.

(make it on page 111)

BUCKLED-UP HEADBOARD

PAGE 74

I was so darned tired of my dated 1980s' metal bed that I avoided the bedroom. I also avoided bringing up the subject of a new one, because I knew how that conversation would go. The only option was a makeover. This was a crazy experiment, but it worked for me (and my budget).

(make it on page 112)

VINYL REVIVAL

PAGE 75

A friend of mine had a little mishap with her groovy turquoise vinyl sectional. The details of the accident are unclear, but it involved a heavy object falling off the wall onto the seat of one of the sections. Aside from the large gash in the vinyl, no injuries were reported, but because of the damage, she sold it to me for a song.

(make it on page 114)

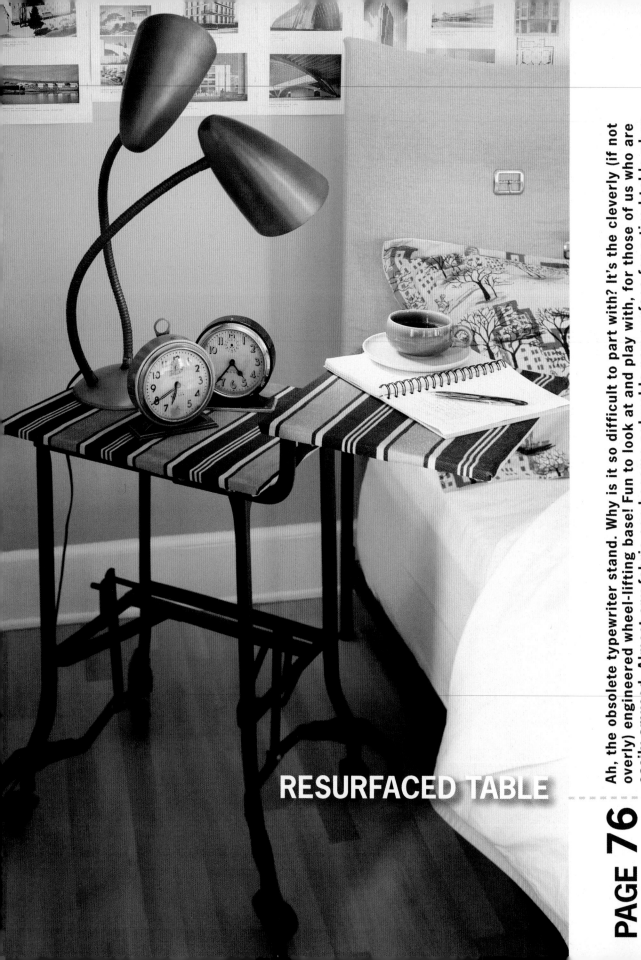

RESURFACED TABLE

Ah, the obsolete typewriter stand. Why is it so difficult to part with? It's the cleverly (if not overly) engineered wheel-lifting base! Fun to look at and play with, for those of us who are easily amused. Almost any fabric can become a durable new surface for a tired table when you apply a few coats of clear polyurethane.

(make it on page 115)

MID-CENTURY TIE CHAIR

PAGE 77

Men just seem to wear lackluster ties these days. I prefer the older styles, so I upholster chairs with them. These vibrant ties give this chair a very hip new look. Trouble is, some guy wearing a very boring tie will end up sitting on it.

(make it on page 116)

HAPPY HANKY STOOL

When disposable tissues came along, I guess handkerchiefs lost their jobs. When I meet up with a lovely, unemployed handkerchief, it makes me a little bit sad, so I bring it home. They need the work, so why not save a tree and make a hanky happy?

(make it on page 118)

SHOPPING CART HAMPER

Even though my neighborhood is pedestrian-friendly, it's extremely rare to witness groceries being wheeled home in one of these smart utility carts. We'd rather use our cars. No longer used as originally intended, then, this little cart is outfitted with a vintage barkcloth liner and is reincarnated as a charming container for large quantities of dirty laundry.

(make it on page 120)

make it

A little disclaimer here: my upholstery skills are basically self-taught, so the instructional approach in certain cases is not necessarily the same as those a "real professional" might take. My methods have served me well and continue to get the job done, which assures me that they will also work for you.

Most of the projects revolve around found objects, and more than likely your found objects will differ from mine. This may mean that you won't always be able to follow the "recipes" exactly. Don't despair. Some trial and error might be necessary as you adapt to the differences. Mistakes often lead to discovery and may spawn a genius idea for your next great project.

embellished lanterns

SEE P 45

GET

Needle-nose pliers

Scissors

Lanterns with removable glass

Scarf bits, or other translucent fabric remnants

Double-sided clear tape

DO

1 Use needle-nose pliers to bend back the metal tabs that hold the glass in place on the lantern, and carefully remove each glass panel.

2 Cut the fabric remnants to the same size as the glass panels.

3 Apply double-sided tape to the perimeter of the right side of the glass.

4 Pull the cut remnants tautly over the glass, while pressing them into place on the tape.

note

As you may have noticed, I snuck a little pattern tissue into the mix. I often recycle paper items in my work for a little variety.

bend metal tabs to remove glass panels

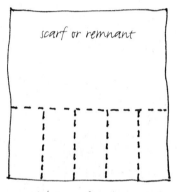

cut fabric to fit glass panels

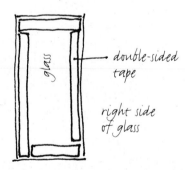

sanctuary chair

SEE P 46

GET

Tool kit (page 123)

Small flat-head screwdriver

Needle-nose pliers

Staple gun and staples

Hot glue gun and glue sticks

Old chair with removable seat cushion

Towel, gently used

Decorative 1-inch-wide trim, 1½ yards

30 to 40 decorative furniture nails (optional)

DO

1 Remove the cushion from the chair; it's usually a plywood cutout topped with foam and secured to the frame with screws. Remove the existing fabric from the cushion. To do this, you may need to pry the tacks or staples from the underside using a small flat-head screwdriver and needle-nose pliers. Use the old fabric as a guide to cut the new piece from one end of the towel. (Just follow the basic shape of the cushion, but add at least 2 inches all around.) Pull the towel tightly over the cushion, and staple the raw edges to the underside. Clip the curves as needed to make a tight fit.

2 From the remainder of the towel, cut a piece 2 inches larger than the opening in the back of the chair. Stretch this piece across the opening and secure it with staples along the perimeter. Trim the excess fabric. Use the hot glue gun to apply the decorative trim, covering the staples and raw edges.

3 Using decorative furniture nails for a nailhead trim (see page 126) is optional. If you want to add the nails, begin by placing one at each of the four corners first. Use a tape measure to mark off evenly spaced intervals between the four corners, and place the remaining nails over the marks. The decorative nails on the chair shown are placed about 2 inches apart, but this distance itself isn't important as long as it remains consistent.

step 1

step 2

note

This chair's back is like a window frame, meaning the view from the back is the reverse side of the towel. If you prefer a different look, you can address this by repeating steps 2 and 3 on the back. If your towel isn't large enough to cover this additional area, a coordinating remnant can be substituted.

If your towel has fringed ends, here's an idea. Add a little flourish by trimming them off (½ inch beyond the edge of the fringe, to keep the fringe intact) and gluing them to the underside of the seat's perimeter.

mod garment rack screen

SEE P 47

DO

1 Measure the span between the top and bottom rods of the rack and add about 6 inches, as shown. Cut the full width of the fabric to this length. (The size of the rods may vary per rack, so make sure 6 extra inches is enough to wrap around the rods at both ends.)

2 Fold over 3 inches at each end, and stitch to form two casings.

3 Dismantle the rack to free the rods. Slide the rods through the casings, and reconnect them to the rack.

GET

Tool kit (page 123)

Free standing garment rack (one of those lightweight racks that you can dismantle, designed for the storage of seasonal or overflow clothing)

Fabric, 2 yards (see **note**)

Seam allowance is ½ inch, unless otherwise noted.

note

Fabric that is 54 to 60 inches wide will be wider than the average garment rack, which results in attractive gathers at the top and bottom of the rack. A narrow rack might only need 45-inch-wide fabric. Experiment to see what works. Leave the selvages in place for the sides, so there is no need for a hem.

step 1

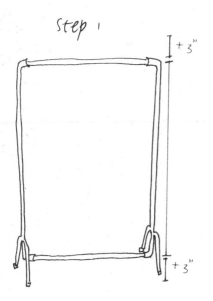

+ 3"

+ 3"

step 2

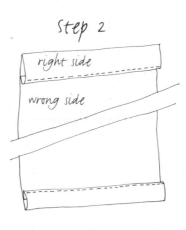

right side

wrong side

step 3

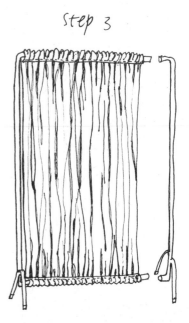

window bench cushion

SEE P 48

GET

Tool kit (page 123)

Newspaper

Tape, clear or masking

Felt pen

Electric knife (Some foam suppliers will cut the foam to size if you provide a template; most often they will make only one cut, and then you're on your own.)

Spray adhesive

Foam, medium density, 3 to 4 inches thick, enough to fit the spot you have in mind

High-loft 100 percent polyester batting (enough to wrap around the foam)

Medium to heavyweight upholstery fabric (I used heavyweight linen. To figure out how much fabric you need, get out your tape measure and consult page 127.)

Extra long zipper (For a rehab cushion, it makes sense to reuse the zipper. If you can't, purchase a roll of "endless" zipper as described on page 124.)

Welt cording, enough to go around the entire cushion twice

Seam allowance is ½ inch, unless otherwise noted.

DO

1 Use the newspaper, scissors, and tape (if needed) to make a pattern of the area your cushion will cover. Trace your pattern onto the foam with the felt pen.

2 Use the electric knife to cut the foam, following the outside edge of the line. Keep the knife as straight as possible (perpendicular to the top and bottom surfaces) as you cut.

3 To soften and round out the cushion, cover the foam with batting. First lay the batting on top and cut it to the length of the cushion. Then wrap it over the front edge and around the bottom of the foam, and trim to size, as shown. Lift up the batting one side at a time, apply the spray adhesive to the foam, and replace the batting.

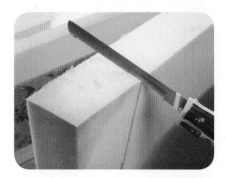

4 Fold your fabric with the right sides facing, and pin the newspaper pattern (the one you used for cutting foam) to both layers. Before you cut, add ½ inch all around for seam allowance.

note

Before you attempt making a cushion from scratch, I suggest that you first replace the cover on an existing cushion. Sometimes the best way to learn how to construct something is to take it apart. If you do it carefully, you can use the old fabric as a pattern for your new cover.

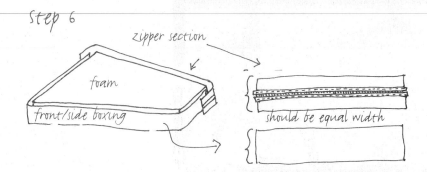

step 6

zipper section

foam

front/side boxing

should be equal width

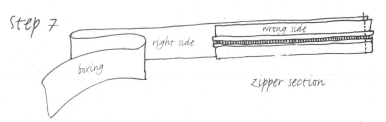

step 7

right side

wrong side

boxing

zipper section

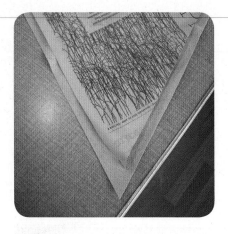

5 To make the front/side boxing:

• For the width, cut a strip that is ¾ inch wider than the depth of the foam. Ordinarily you would add 1 inch (for two ½-inch seam allowances). But by skimping a bit on that measurement, and still stitching ½-inch seams, the cover will be a snug fit on the cushion. After all, who wants baggy cushion covers?

• The length of the boxing strip should be enough to cover both sides and the front of the cushion. For example, if the foam is 20 x 36 x 4 inches, the boxing should measure 76 x 4¾ inches.

• If you have any graphic elements to add as decoration, simply stitch them onto the front/side boxing strip as desired. Have some fun with it!

6 To make the zipper portion of the boxing and put it all together:

• The zipper portion should be about 4 inches longer than the length of the cushion, so it will extend a bit around the back corners. (For example, if the cushion is 36 inches long, the zipper portion should be 40 inches long.) This will make the cover much easier to stuff when finished.

• You will need to cut two strips of fabric for the zipper portion. To determine the width of these strips, add 1 inch to the width of the front/side boxing (step 5) and divide by 2.

• Baste the two strips together lengthwise with right sides facing. Open the seam and install the zipper as you normally would. The width of the zipper portion should now equal the width of the front/side boxing, as shown.

7 With right sides facing, stitch one end of the long boxing strip to the closed end of the zipper portion. The other end will be stitched later, so leave it alone for now.

8 To make the cording, see page 126.

To attach the cording to the top and the bottom pieces:

• Use the zipper foot of your sewing machine, with the needle set to the left side.

• Pin the cording to the perimeter, on the right side. Start at the center back, about 3 inches from the end of the cording, as shown.

• Keep raw edges aligned and the needle as close to the cording as possible as you pass it through the machine.

• When you reach a corner, make a few cuts in the cording as shown, to make the turn easier.

• Stop stitching when you are about 6 inches from the starting point. Lay the fabric flat and the cording ends side by side. Make sure the two ends overlap by at least 1 inch, and cut.

• Stitch the ends of the cording as instructed on page 126.

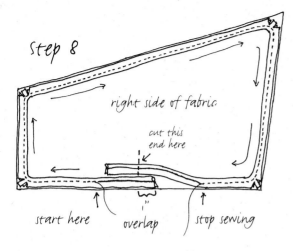

step 8

right side of fabric

cut this end here

start here   overlap   stop sewing

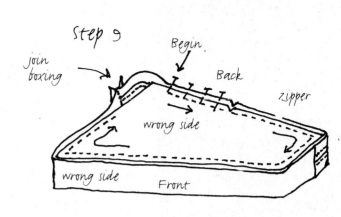

step 9

join boxing

Begin

Back

zipper

wrong side

wrong side   Front

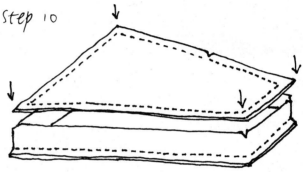

step 10

9 Start the cover assembly with the back piece:

• Make a notch at the center back on both the top and bottom pieces, as shown. Also, make a notch on both sides at the center of the zipper portion.

• With right sides facing, match the notch at the center back of the corded section with the notch at the center of the zipper section. The remainder of the boxing strip will become the cushion front.

• Pin the two sections together between the zipper's start and the center notches. Begin stitching as shown (the corded section should be on the top side).

• It is very important to stitch as close to the cording as possible. You may need to apply pressure with your left hand as you stitch to accomplish this.

• Continue stitching until you are about 6 inches from where you began.

• With right sides facing, stitch the two ends of the boxing strip together. You may have to make an adjustment in the length of the strip at this point to match the remaining span. Continue stitching where you left off.

10 Make small notches (keep them well within the seam allowance) on the boxing strip, directly opposite each stitched corner. This is to mark exactly where the corners are, so you can accurately line up the corners of the top piece with the corners of the bottom piece. Pin the remaining corded section to the boxing strip, again with the right sides facing and the corded section on the top. Make sure to match the corners to the notches. Stitch all the way around.

11 Open the zipper and stuff the cushion with the foam, making sure the batting-free face of the foam is at the back. (It's so annoying when the zipper gets stuck in the batting.) Make sure all the seam allowances are facing the same direction. Also, it may be necessary to add a little extra batting to fill out the corners. Good luck! Sometimes stuffing a cushion is a lot like wrestling an alligator.

scarf lampshade

SEE P 49

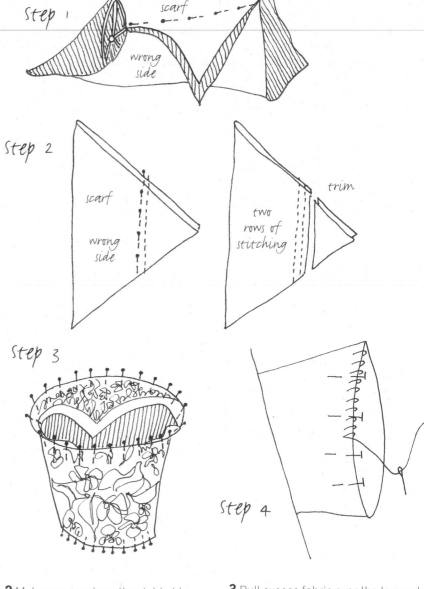

step 1

scarf

wrong side

step 2

scarf

wrong side

two rows of stitching

trim

step 3

step 4

GET

Tool kit (page 123)

Embroidery needle (large eye)

Large lightweight vintage scarf

Small lampshade frame (strip the fabric from an old damaged shade)

Embroidery floss, narrow ribbon, or cord

Seam allowance is ½ inch, unless otherwise noted.

DO

1 Lay the lampshade frame on the right side of the scarf at a diagonal (the scarf's bias). Bring the opposing corners together, pulling lightly around the frame, as shown, and pin where the scarf meets. Since you are working on the scarf's bias, it should stretch to follow the contours of the lampshade. Carefully slip the scarf off the top of the frame without removing the pins.

2 Make a seam along the right side of the row of pins. Remove the pins and make another seam parallel to this one about ¼ inch to the inside, as shown. Trim away excess fabric. Turn the fabric right-side out and slip it over the frame. If the scarf doesn't fit tightly, remove it and make another seam parallel to and slightly inside the previous seam. It's hard to get this right the first time. Sometimes ⅛ inch is all you need to get it nice and tight. Just add ⅛ inch at a time until you're satisfied with the fit, then align the seam with one of the vertical bars of the frame.

3 Pull excess fabric over the top and bottom of the frame, stretching tightly as you do so, and pin the scarf in place.

4 With the embroidery needle and floss, sew the scarf to the top and bottom of the frame using a slipstitch. Cut away excess fabric.

note

To avoid the risk of your handiwork going up in smoke, please use a low-watt bulb (40 or less) with your scarf lampshade.

GET

Tool kit (page 123)

Screwdriver

Staple gun and staples (or upholstery tacks and hammer if you feel like pounding)

Chairs with removable seats

Printed canvas, enough to cover the number of chairs you're tackling

DO

1 Release the chair seats by removing the screws from the underside.

2 Assess whether or not it's necessary to remove the existing fabric. If it's mildewed or has an unpleasant odor, you may want to ditch it. Otherwise, it's perfectly fine to upholster right over it.

3 Measure from beneath the seat, across the top, and around/beneath to the other side. Do this in both directions. Cut the canvas large enough to wrap around the seat and tack to the base underneath.

4 On a sturdy work surface, place the canvas right side down and center the chair seat facedown over the canvas. Pull the edges of the canvas over to the backside, and staple (or tack) it in place. It's best to staple methodically, placing the first staple at the center front. Pull the canvas taut, and place the second staple directly opposite the first at the center back. Repeat this procedure in the opposite direction (side to side), as shown.

5 Continue working in this manner, from the center of each side toward the corners, pulling the canvas taut before you staple. Fold the corners flat in a V shape, as shown in the diagram, and staple the folded edges.

6 Replace the seat in its frame, and replace the screws.

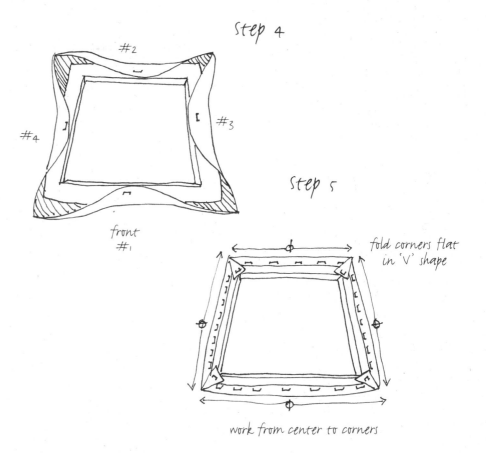

step 4

#2

#3

#4

front
#1

step 5

fold corners flat
in 'V' shape

work from center to corners

ball fringe
footstool slipcover

SEE P 51

GET

Tool kit (page 123)

Zipper foot (optional)

Footstool, small to medium size

Fabric remnant, 1 yard

Backing material to match
ball fringe

Ball fringe, 28 yards

Thread, matching color

Brush fringe in contrasting color,
about 3 yards (optional)

*Seam allowance is ½ inch, unless
otherwise noted.*

note

Material amounts are estimated and will
vary depending on the size of the footstool.

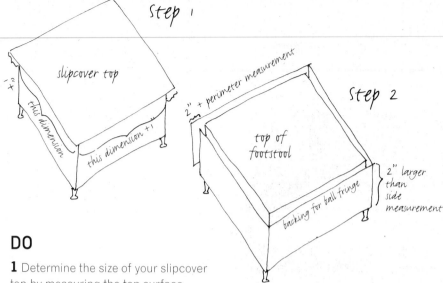

step 1

slipcover top

2" +

this dimension

this dimension +1

step 2

2" + perimeter measurement

top of
footstool

backing for ball fringe

2" larger
than
side
measurement

DO

1 Determine the size of your slipcover
top by measuring the top surface
of the existing footstool. Add 1 inch
to both dimensions to get the size
of the top piece, as shown. (The
footstool shown here measures
25 x 25 inches, so I cut the
top piece to 26 x 26 inches.)

2 To find the length of the ball fringe
backing:

• Add together the length of all four
sides, and add 2 inches to that number. (Ordinarily, you would add just 1
inch here for two seam allowances,
but stitching so much weight to the
backing causes it to cinch up a bit.)

For the width:

• Measure the height of the upholstered side, and add 2 inches to that
number, as shown. (The perimeter of
my footstool measured 100 inches and
the sides measured 7 inches, so I cut
my backing piece 102 x 9 inches.) It's
fine to stitch together shorter strips of
the backing material to reach the correct length. Zigzag or serge the raw
edges of the cut pieces.

3 Stitch the ball fringe to one edge
of the backing strip along its entire
length. The first row of fringe will
become the bottom edge of the slipcover. When you reach the end, cut
the fringe and return to the other end
to attach an adjacent row, as shown.
Nest the balls closely together as you
stitch, to form a honeycomb pattern.
Continue stitching rows of ball fringe
until you have covered the entire
backing strip.

step 3 (detail)

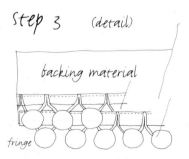

backing material

fringe

step 4

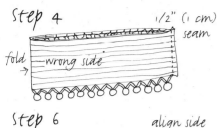

½" (1 cm) seam
fold → wrong side

step 6

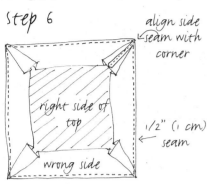

align side seam with corner

right side of top

wrong side

½" (1 cm) seam

4 With right sides together, stitch the short ends of the ball fringe strip ½ inch from the edge, as shown. You may have to cut out a few balls in order to feed it through the machine. A zipper foot will also help.

5 If you want to include a contrasting brush fringe, now is the time to add it. Lay the slipcover top out flat, right side facing up. With right sides facing, align the bound flat edge of the fringe with the edge of the top, pinning it around the entire perimeter (the fringe will lay on the slipcover top, not hang over the edge). Overlap the ends by a bit. Machine-baste the flat edge to the top piece, pivoting at the corners.

6 With right sides together, pin the top edge of the puffball strip to the perimeter of the top piece (on top of the brush fringe, if added in step 4). Position the side seam to line up with one of the corners, as shown. Stitch ½ inch from the edge on all four sides, pivoting at the corners. Take care not to catch the brush fringe in the stitches. Clip the corners.

7 Turn the piece right side out, and slip it over the footstool.

scarf-striped curtain

SEE P 52

GET

Tool kit (page 123)

Tab-top curtain

Rectangular vintage scarves

Thread, coordinating color

Seam allowance is ½ inch, unless otherwise noted.

DO

1 Cut the curtain off at the desired place.

2 Fold the cut edge toward the right side of the fabric by about ½ inch, and stitch as shown. Since the curtains already have a finished edge on the sides (usually either a hem or a selvage), there is no need to hem the sides.

3 Pin and then topstitch a scarf to the hemmed edge of the curtain, covering the raw edge as shown. This method allows both sides of the curtain to have a finished look.

4 Hem another section of the curtain as in step 2, and repeat step 3 with another scarf.

5 Add more sections as needed until you have the intended length.

step 2

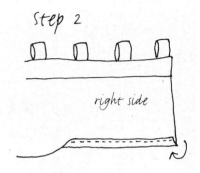

right side

step 3

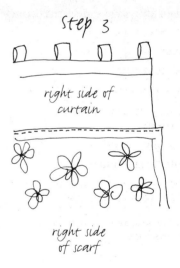

right side of curtain

right side of scarf

note

If you're not as lucky as I was, and the length of your scarf doesn't happen to match up with the width of your curtain, simply turn both ends of the scarf toward the wrong side and stitch a single-fold hem, as shown below.

wrong side

SEE P 53

GET

Tool kit (page 123)

Vacuum cleaner!

24-inch ruler or yardstick

Felt-tip marker

Heavy-duty sewing machine needle

Large hand-sewing needle

Well-worn fur coats, a couple (check your mother-in-law's closet, maybe)

72-inch wide felt (for the backing), 1½ yards

Fringe for border (I recycled the edging from an old tablecloth.)

Seam allowance is ½ inch, unless otherwise noted.

DO

1 Remove the linings from the coats. Cut off the sleeves and collars, and open the seams to create flat pieces of fur. (This is where the vacuum becomes essential. Fur will fly into every area of your house, not to mention eyes, nose, and throat). Remove all hooks-and-eyes and buttons.

2 On the wrong side of the hide, mark off the largest square or rectangle you can make from each piece of fur, as shown, and cut them out.

3 Pin the fur pieces to the felt backing, right-side up and edge to edge. Using a very wide stitch setting, stitch ¼ inch from the edge of each hide piece. It helps to "part" the fur as you feed it through the machine. If you begin in the center of the felt backing and work toward each end, it will min-imize the amount of fabric that has to pass inside the arm of your sewing machine (the most difficult part of this project—well, aside from the fur aspiration). I arranged my fur pieces in a checkerboard pattern because I had two very different colored minks. Feel free to design your own throw. If you don't have enough fur to cover the area of the felt, just cut the felt smaller. No rules.

4 Keep stitching until the felt is covered. Trim the felt backing as needed to make it even with the top. Use a very large needle or other pointed object to pick the fur out from under the topstitching, to camouflage the seams. Topstitch the trim to the outer edges of the throw, mitering at the corners.

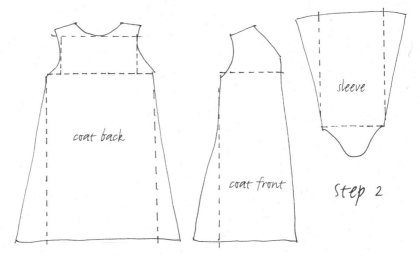

coat back

coat front

sleeve

step 2

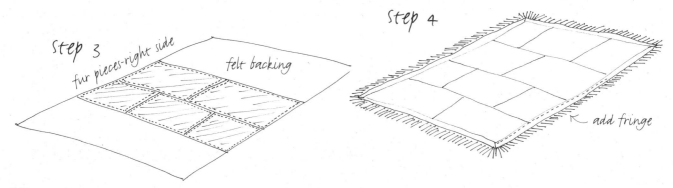

step 3

fur pieces-right side

felt backing

step 4

add fringe

wool coat bolster

SEE P 54

GET

Tool kit (page 123)

Old long coat

Body pillow, 18 x 50 inches

54-inch-wide fabric (for pillow back), ¾ yard

Seam allowance is ½ inch, unless otherwise noted.

DO

1 Use a seam ripper to open the seam at the center back of the coat. Lay the buttoned coat flat, with the right side facing up, as shown.

2 At the coat's midsection, mark off and cut a rectangle measuring 22 x 54 inches.

3 Cut a 22 x 54-inch rectangle from the fabric you've chosen for the pillow back.

4 With right sides facing, pin and stitch the two sections together on all four sides, pivoting at the corners. Clip all four corners.

5 Unbutton the coat, and turn it right-side out. Use a point turner to push out the corners, and press.

steps 1 and 2

6 Stitch a 1½-inch flange around the perimeter (see page 125).

7 Insert the body pillow through the coat opening, and button it up.

---

scrappy table linens

SEE P 55

GET

Tool kit (page 123)

Linen remnants

Trims of your choice

Printed cloth (such as moneybags, feed sacks, work aprons, etc.)

DO

1 Gather up some linen scraps of different sizes, and cut them into appropriate (desired) shapes. Larger pieces can become towels; smaller pieces will work for dinner or cocktail napkins. The sizes don't have to be consistent. (Only five-year-olds care if the person sitting next to them has a bigger napkin.)

2 Hem the edges of the linen. Stitch on your favorite trims, if you wish.

3 Snip the letters from the printed cloth, and start the word search!

4 Pin the words to the towels and napkins wherever and however you choose, and stitch them on. I attached mine with lots of back and forth stitching, leaving the edges raw to ravel after washing. I think zigzag stitching would look fun, too.

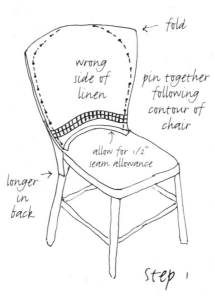

hemstitched linens slipcover

SEE P 56

GET

Tool kit (page 123)

Tape

Bow-back chair

2 vintage linens, approximately 20 x 40 inches

Old sheer curtain panel

Zipper (optional)

Seam allowance is ½ inch, unless otherwise noted.

DO

1 Drape one of the linens over the back of the chair with the wrong side facing out. Pin the edges together following the contour of the chair, as shown. Allow ½ inch (where the front end meets the seat) for seam allowance, and let the opposite longer end fall naturally at the back. If your linen is much wider than the chair, just trim off what you don't need. Remove the linen from the chair and stitch along the line of pins. Trim the corners at the fold.

2 Center the second linen over the seat, wrong side facing down, and use tape to hold it in place. Use fabric chalk or a pencil to mark the outline of the seat onto the linen. Cut ½ inch outside the line for seam allowance. Save the two decorative ends for constructing the short skirt.

3 With right sides facing, pin the linen seat to the front of the linen back, and stitch.

4 To make the short skirt:

• With right sides facing, pin the cut edge of the decorative ends to the perimeter of the seat, with the ends meeting in the center front, then stitch. Pin and then stitch the linen back to the short skirt at each side. Turn the skirt right side out, and press the seams.

5 To determine the amount of sheer fabric you'll need for the underskirt, measure the perimeter of the bottom edge of the slipcover and multiply by 3. The sheer skirt shown is about 12 inches long and has an unfinished hem (about 2 inches above the floor). Tear as many 12-inch-wide lengths as you need from the old curtain sheer, and stitch them together to fulfill the required measurement. Tearing this type of synthetic fabric is very accurate and causes the edges to curl naturally into an attractive unfinished hem.

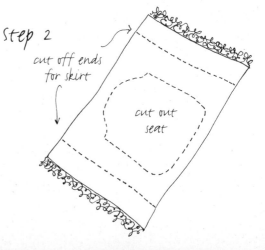

step 4

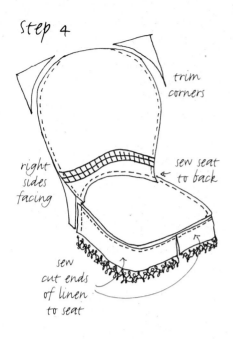

trim corners

right sides facing

sew seat to back

sew cut ends of linen to seat

6 Make successive 1-inch tucks in the fabric, as shown, as you baste the top edge of the skirt. Flatten the pleats with a cool iron. Starting at the center front of the slipcover's short skirt, pin and then stitch the sheer skirt to the underside.

7 Closure options: Install a short zipper at the center front of the skirt. It's impossible for me to resist the opportunity for a seductive detail, especially when it's front and center. If you don't want to fuss with a zipper, you could try a loop and button closure, using a length of narrow ribbon and a lovely vintage button. Or, it's fine to take the easy way out and just stitch the opening closed.

baste tucks in sheer skirt length

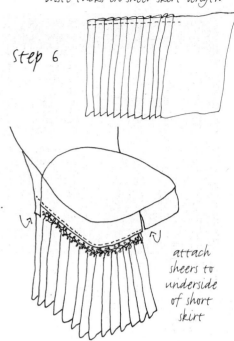

step 6

attach sheers to underside of short skirt

GET

Tool kit (page 123)

Three or more vintage full-ruffled slips

A single bed in need of love

Inexpensive cotton fabric or an old flat bedsheet

Seam allowance is ½ inch, unless otherwise noted.

DO

1 Cut each slip at one side seam and open it flat. By holding one up to the bed, you can determine the length you'd like the skirt to be, measuring from the top of the box spring to an inch or two above the floor. Trim the excess length from the top of the slip, adding ½ inch for seam allowance, as shown. Trim additional slips to the same length.

2 Measure the length and width of the top of the box spring, which is usually 39 x 75 inches. Add 3 inches to the length (for a hem at the top end), and cut the cotton fabric or old bedsheet to this size. Make a wide double-fold hem by pressing the top edge under ½ inch, then press under another 2½ inches. Stitch the edge of the hem in place.

3 Starting at the front end, with right sides facing, pin the raw edges of the slips to the perimeter of the piece that will cover the box spring. Stitch in the same direction. When you reach the end of one slip, simply continue with another. No need to sew the slips together, because the flounce will camouflage the gaps. Continue along three sides as shown. Trim the two corners, and press the seam allowances to the underside of the box spring cover.

4 Arrange the bed skirt over the box spring, and place the mattress on top of it.

step 3

right sides facing

step 1

open flat

trim to desired length from top

cut open at side seam

bowtie handle variation

GET

Tool kit (page 123)

2 obis, one approximately 11 inches wide, and one approximately 6 inches wide

2 bowties (the real kind, not the cheaters)

Bias tape, coordinating color, 1¼ yards (optional)

Seam allowance is ½ inch, unless otherwise noted.

DO

1 Cut two 15-inch lengths from each obi. Lay out one of the 6-inch-wide obi strips, right side facing up, and mark the center point with pins. Pin the ends of the bow ties, right side up, about 2½ inches on either side of the center. Overlap the contrasting obi piece along the pinned edge, with the ends of the ties tucked in between the two layers. Pin together and topstitch ⅛ inch from the edge. For a nice touch, add another row of topstitching about ¼ inch from the first. Repeat with the remaining obi pieces to make the other side of the tote.

2 With the right sides facing, stitch both sides of the tote together at the sides and bottom.

3 With right sides facing, pull out the bottom corners. Align the side seams with the bottom seam as shown, with seam allowances open and lying flat. Stitch across and perpendicular to these seams about 3 inches from the corner. Trim off the corners, and bind the seams with bias tape, if desired.

belt handle variation

GET

Tool kit (page 123)

2 obis, one approximately 11 inches wide, and one approximately 6 inches wide

2 cloth-covered belts, at least 1 inch wide

Bias tape, coordinating color, 1¼ yards (optional)

Seam allowance is ½ inch, unless otherwise noted.

DO

1 Cut two 18-inch lengths from each obi. Overlap the obis along the longest edges, as shown. Pin together and topstitch ⅛ inch from the edge. Do the same for both sides of the tote, and mark the center point of each seam and top edge with pins.

2 Cut one 7-inch length from the narrow obi to make a pocket. Turn the raw edges under, and baste. Center and pin the pocket to the wrong side of one section, about 1½ inches from the top edge. Stitch in place.

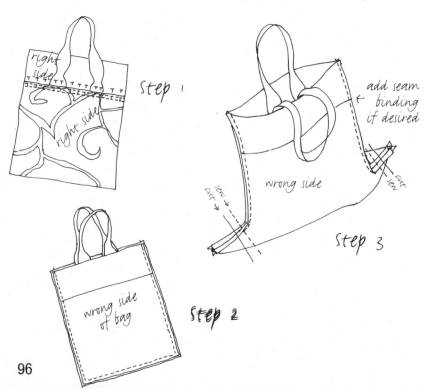

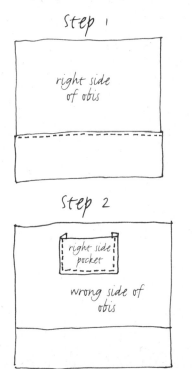

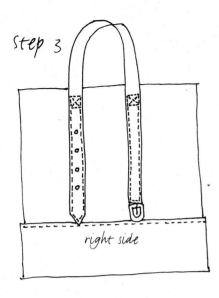

step 3

right side

3 Pin the belt to the right side of the fabric about 3 inches on either side of the center, leaving a loop about 7 inches beyond the top edge. Stitch the belt into place as shown. Reinforce the stitching near the top edge with a box stitch. Repeat with the second belt on the other side of the tote.

4 Pin the sections with the right sides facing, and stitch together at sides and bottom.

5 To finish the bottom corners and seams, follow directions in step 3 of the Bowtie Handle Tote with this one change: Stitch 2 inches from the corner rather than 3 inches.

vintage bike seat

GET

Tool kit (page 123)

Bike seat

Vintage barkcloth, ½ yard

¼-inch elastic, ½ yard

DO

1 Lay the fabric over the seat with at least ½ inch of overhang at the bottom edge. Pin the fabric to the seat on all sides. Trim the fabric ½ inch from the lower edge as shown, following the shape of the seat.

2 Pin tucks, where necessary, to help the fabric conform to the contours of the seat. When you're satisfied, top-stitch the tucks.

3 Stitch the elastic to the right side of the fabric around the perimeter of the seat cover. To gather the fabric sufficiently, pull the elastic toward you and stretch it to the full extent as you sew.

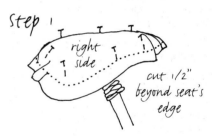

step 1

right side

cut 1/2" beyond seat's edge

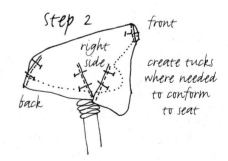

step 2

front

right side

back

create tucks where needed to conform to seat

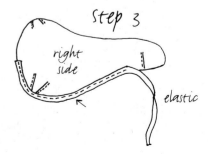

step 3

right side

elastic

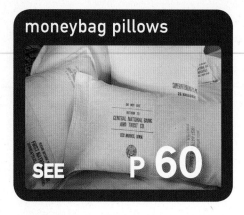
GET

Tool kit (page 123)

Washing machine

Detergent

Pillow forms (size will vary according to bag sizes)

Cotton moneybags

Extra fabric for pillow backs (remnants or inexpensive cotton will do)

Zippers to match (or not to match, who cares?) (optional)

Seam allowance is ½ inch, unless otherwise noted.

DO

1 Machine-wash the bags using ordinary detergent. Dry.

2 Using the seam ripper, open the seams of the bags and press them flat. Take measurements of the open bags to determine the size of pillow forms you will need. For example, to cover a 16 inch pillow, your canvas will need to be at least 17 inches square. (To make larger pillows, you may need to sew two bags together and then adjust the shape to fit the pillow form.)

3 To install a zipper, cut the fabric for your pillow back 1 inch longer than the pillow front fabric. Cut a 4-inch strip from one end of the longer side.

4 With right sides together, join the two pieces by basting a ½-inch seam along this cut. Press the seam open. Install a centered zipper that is about 6 inches shorter than the width of the pillow back. (This is to allow for a 2-inch or narrower flange. If your pillow will not have a flange, the zipper can be up to 1 inch shorter than the pillow back.) Remove the basting stitches along the length of the zipper.

5 Open the zipper at least an inch (to make it easier to turn the pillow cover right side out), then pin and stitch the pillow front and back together. Clip the corners, fully open the zipper, and turn the cover right side out.

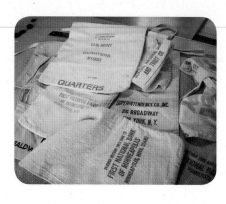

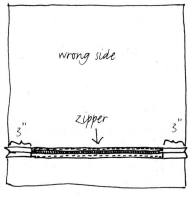

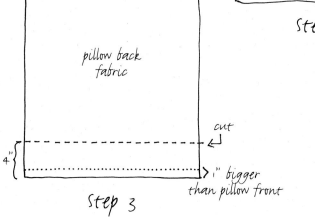

wrong side

zipper

3"   3"

step 4

pillow back fabric

cut

4"

1" bigger than pillow front

step 3

note

Most of my pillows feature something I really like on the front, and I save on cost by using remnants on the back. So I often choose the easy split-back construcion. If you'd like to do this too, measure and cut the money bags to size, and then refer to steps 3 thru 6 of the Vintage Scarf Pillow instructions on page 102 to complete the pillows.

GET

Tool kit (page 123)

Old couch

Zippers (reuse the old zippers or buy new ones the same length)

Upholstery needle, 7 inches or longer

Filler fabric (the fabric that won't show, under the bottom cushion)

Upholstery fabric

12 neckties (approximately)

Covered button kit with 10 buttons

Welt cording, enough to surround the cushions' top and bottom edges

Waxed string

Seam allowance is ½ inch, unless otherwise noted.

note

material amounts will vary depending on the size of the couch (see page 127)

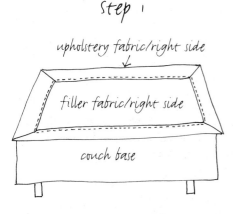

step 1

upholstery fabric/right side

filler fabric/right side

couch base

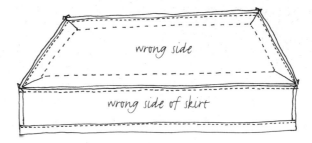

step 3

wrong side

wrong side of skirt

DO

1 To make a slipcover for the base:

• First, remove the loose cushions and measure the area of the base of the couch. Cut a section of the filler fabric that is 1 inch larger than the area.

• Cut four 5-inch-wide strips from the upholstery fabric: two strips should be the length of the sides and two strips should be the length of the front and back of the filler fabric section.

• Machine-baste a ½-inch hem along one long edge of each strip. Pin the strips to the right side of the filler fabric section, covering 4½ inches of the outside edge, and topstitch them in place. You can miter the strips at each corner, but it is not necessary.

2 Cut four pieces from the upholstery fabric to create the "skirt" section.

• To determine the width of the skirt pieces, measure the distance from the top edge of the couch base to the floor. To this measurement, add ½ inch for the seam allowance and 2½ inches for the hem.

• To determine the length, add 1 inch to the length of the front/back of the couch and add 1 inch to the length of the sides.

3 With right sides facing, stitch the skirt sections together at all four corners. Along the edge that will be the bottom, press under ½ inch, then press under 2 inches. Stitch the double-fold hem. With right sides facing, pin the skirt to the top portion of the slipcover as shown, matching the seams with the corners. Stitch the two sections together along the entire perimeter. Turn the piece right side out. Press the seams, and place the cover over the base of the couch.

4 To make the necktie cording, open the seams at the back of the neckties and remove the interfacing. Cut off about 4 inches from the wide ends of 10 neckties, and put them aside for making the covered buttons. Cut the neckties lengthwise into 2-inch strips. To construct the cording, refer to page 126.

5 If you are re-covering existing cushions, simply remove the old fabric and carefully deconstruct it. Use the old pieces as patterns to cut out the new cover. To make new cushions from scratch, and for instructions on stitching the cushion covers, refer to steps 5 through 11 of the Window Bench Cushion on page 86.

6 To make the covered buttons, follow the manufacturer's directions on the button kit. For directions on how to attach the buttons to the cushion, refer to steps 7 and 8 of the Buckled-Up Headboard on page 112. Pull the waxed string from one side of the cushion to the other side, as shown.

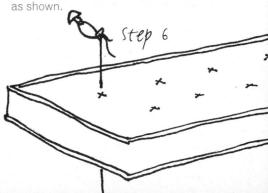

step 6

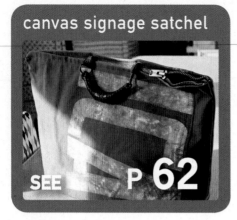
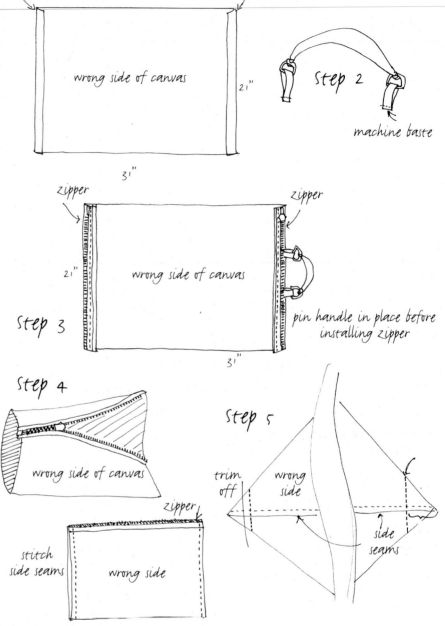

step 1

fold

fold and press

wrong side of canvas

21"

31"

step 2

machine baste

zipper

zipper

21"

wrong side of canvas

step 3

pin handle in place before installing zipper

31"

step 4

wrong side of canvas

zipper

stitch side seams

wrong side

step 5

trim off

wrong side

side seams

GET

Tool kit (page 123)

Heavy-duty sewing machine needle

Canvas, enough to cut a 21 x 31-inch rectangle

1-inch coordinating twill tape, 8 inches long

Salvaged leather handle with D-rings attached

Chunky separating zipper, 20 inches long

Heavy-duty thread, matching color

Seam allowance is ½ inch, unless otherwise noted.

DO

1 Cut a 21 x 31-inch rectangle from the canvas. The 21-inch ends will become the top of the satchel. In preparation for installing the zipper, fold the top edges over about 1 inch, with wrong sides facing, and press flat as shown.

2 Cut the 8-inch length of twill tape into two 4-inch lengths. Loop each one through the D-rings of the handle and machine-baste the ends together, as shown. Center the handle at one of the top edges, and pin the twill tape to the canvas.

3 Separate the zipper, and pin each length facedown on the folds, aligning the teeth with the folded edge, as shown. The zipper will lie over the handle tabs that you placed in step 2.

4 Reconnect and close the zipper with the wrong side of the canvas facing out (the zipper's tab and the handle will be inside the canvas "tube"). Flatten the tube with the zipper at the top. Align and pin the side edges together and stitch, as shown.

5 To give the bag a flat bottom, pull out the bottom corners, and lay the bag flat. Draw a line 3 inches from the point, perpendicular to the side seams. Stitch along this line, across the side seams. Cut off the triangular corners ½ inch from the seam.

6 Turn the (finished!) bag right side out.

note

The length of the zipper is a determining factor when it comes to designing this bag. If you prefer a larger size bag, use a longer zipper. Add 1 inch to the length of the zipper to determine the width of the canvas. For proportions that are similar to this bag, add 10 inches to that, and you have the length. For example, a 24-inch zipper would require the canvas be cut to 25 x 35 inches. Just make sure the handle you choose will work for the size of the bag.

tip

Strip your worn-out items of their working parts before you send them off to the landfill.

The handle for this bag was salvaged from a badly mildewed vintage suitcase. I kept the handle because it fit my hand so comfortably, and I liked the broken-in look of the leather.

embellished wire basket

SEE **P 63**

GET

Old metal wire locker or bicycle basket

Measuring tapes, cloth or metal

Cloth-cutting scissors (if using cloth tapes)

Old scissors or tin snips (if using metal tapes)

Hot glue gun and glue sticks (if using cloth tapes)

Duct tape (if using metal tapes)

DO

1 Obviously, you'll have to find a basket, if there's not one already lurking in your basement or garage. They are a common find at garage sales; just keep your eyes peeled.

2 Beginning at the top, weave the tape through the first row of the wire grid, all the way around the basket. When you arrive back where you started from, cut the tape measure to the proper length, allowing the ends to overlap about ½ inch.

3 If using cloth measuring tapes, use the hot glue gun to glue the ends together. If using metal tapes, attach the ends with duct tape.

4 Alternate the placement of the tape with each row, so that it goes behind the wire that was crossed over in the previous row.

5 Keep weaving until, you know, you're done (duh)!

note

You can make these baskets with almost any material imaginable. I've used lengths of fiberglass lampshade material from broken lamps, plastic lawn chair webbing, leather belts, lengths of folded newspaper or magazine pages, and banana peels (just kidding) to name a few. Get crazy.

obi sling chair

SEE **P 64**

GET

Tool kit (page 123)

Small flat-head screwdriver

Needle-nose pliers

Upholstery hammer and tacks
(if dowels are fixed to frame)

Sling chair frame

2 obis

DO

I don't want to insult your intelligence by
going into great detail with this project.
Basically, you just need to remove the damaged seat from the chair's frame, note the
method of attachment, and mimic it. Some
sling chairs have removable dowels that slip
through a casing at each end of the canvas.
The dowels in older sling chairs are often
glued, making them sturdier, but require a
bit more work to replace the seating. In that
case, you will have to tack the fabric to the
frame. Both options are covered here.

If your chair has removable dowels
(you are lucky):

1 Slip the canvas off the dowels.
Open the casing at each end, and cut
the obis to this same length.

2 Pin the obis together (overlapping
as needed to match the width of the
old seat), and topstitch through both
layers. Obis come with finished edges
(love that!) so there is no hemming
involved.

3 Using the old seat as a measurement guide for the width of the
casing, fold each end toward the
backside, and stitch the casing.

4 Insert the dowels into their casings,
and return the seat to its frame.

If your chair has fixed dowels (don't
worry, it's still simple):

1 To release the seat, remove the
fabric tacks along the length of each
dowel at both ends of the chair. Use
the screwdriver and needle-nose pliers to pry them loose. Cut the obis to
the same length as the old seat.

2 Follow step 2, from above.

3 Tack the new seat to the frame in
the same manner as it was before.
Place the tacks about an inch apart.

vintage scarf pillow

SEE **P 65**

GET

Tool kit (page 123)

1 square scarf

Nonwoven interfacing, medium
weight, as large as the scarf

Coordinating plain fabric (use up
some remnants), ¾ yard

1 square pillow form (feathers
are nice)

*Seam allowance is ½ inch, unless
otherwise noted.*

DO

(before you start)

• Choose a scarf that is somewhat sturdy.
A very delicate silk is not suitable for
this project.

• Determine the appropriate size pillow
form to use. If you want your pillow to have
a flange (a floppy border) your pillow form
should be at least 5 inches smaller than
your scarf. For example, if your scarf is
23 inches square, use an 18-inch square
pillow form.

• Scarves often have border designs. It
will enhance your pillow if you can plan for
the width of the flange to match the width
of the border.

1 Begin by pressing your scarf flat, being careful to choose the proper setting on your iron.

2 Cut a piece of interfacing to the exact dimensions of the scarf. Pin the interfacing, edge to edge, to the wrong side of the scarf. Machine-baste ¼ inch from the edge on all four sides.

3 Use the ruler and fabric chalk to mark and cut two rectangles from the plain fabric or remnant you have chosen. These should be equal to the length of the scarf and 3 inches longer than half of the width of the scarf. For example, if you're using a 23-inch square scarf, the rectangles should measure 23 x 14½ inches, as shown.

4 Stitch a double-fold ½-inch hem on one long edge of each rectangle, as shown. Press the hems flat.

5 With right sides facing and hemmed edges overlapping in the center, pin the outside edges of the pillow back to the scarf, as shown. Stitch ½ inch from the edge on all four sides. Clip off each of the four corners to reduce bulk, and turn right-side out. Press the edges flat.

6 Pin the front to the back on all four edges again, this time with the wrong sides facing. With the scarf side up, topstitch 2 inches from the edge around the perimeter to create the flange (see page 125).

tip
Make your own guide for topstitching a width that goes beyond your machine's built-in guide by placing a length of masking tape at the desired distance from the needle.

to determine dimensions of pillow back pieces

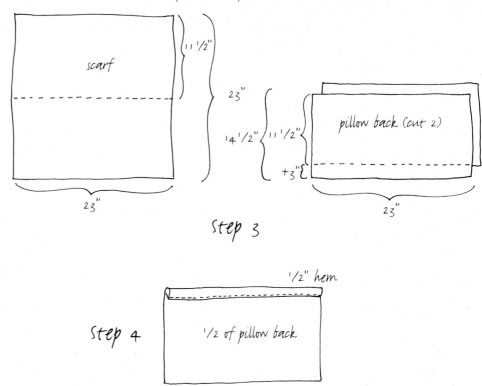

scarf
11½"
23"
14½" { 11½"
+3" {
pillow back (cut 2)
23"
23"

step 3

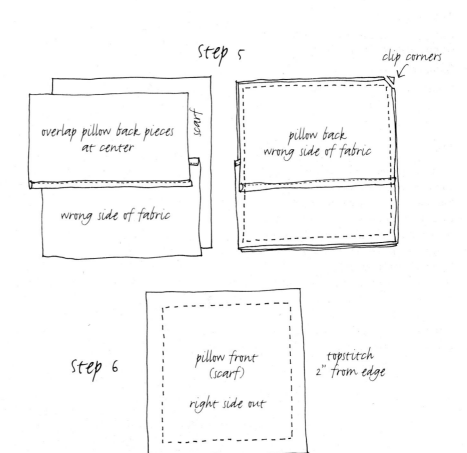

step 4
½" hem
½ of pillow back

step 5
clip corners
overlap pillow back pieces at center
scarf
wrong side of fabric
pillow back wrong side of fabric

step 6
pillow front (scarf)
right side out
topstitch 2" from edge

GET

Tool kit (page 123)

Circular rug

Remnant for bed bottom, enough to duplicate the size and shape of the rug

Burlap or fabric of your choice for the boxing strip, ½ yard

Zipper, 24-inch

Stuffing of your choice (worn-out bed pillows rejected by humans work well, or you can purchase synthetic fiberfill)

Seam allowance is ½ inch, unless otherwise noted.

DO

1 Using the rug as a pattern, as shown, cut the identical shape from the remnant fabric to create the bottom of the bed.

2 Measure the circumference of the rug. To determine the length of the boxing strip, subtract 24 inches (zipper length), and then add 1 inch for seam allowances. The width of the boxing may vary, depending on how thick you want the cushion to be. For the 2½-inch boxing width used in this project, add two ½-inch seam allowances and cut the boxing 3½ inches wide. (For example: if the circumference of the rug is 94 inches, the boxing strip should be cut to 71 x 3½ inches.)

3 To make the zipper portion of the boxing, cut two 25 x 2¾-inch strips from the boxing fabric. Pin and baste the strips together lengthwise, and install the zipper into the seam as you normally would. With right sides facing, pin and stitch each end of the zipper portion to the ends of the main portion of the boxing, as shown, to create a ring.

4 With right sides facing, and the rug on top, pin and stitch the boxing strip to the outer edge of the rug, as shown. Open the zipper slightly and repeat this process to attach the boxing to the bottom piece. Open the zipper fully and turn the dog bed right-side out. Fill with stuffing as desired and close zipper.

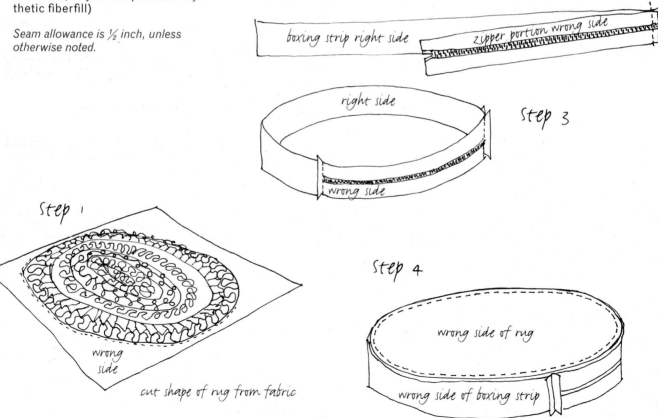

boxing strip right side   zipper portion wrong side

right side

step 3

wrong side

step 1

wrong side

cut shape of rug from fabric

step 4

wrong side of rug

wrong side of boxing strip

giant flowers slipcover

SEE P 67

GET

Tool kit (page 123)

Armless chair

1 blanket or twin-size bedspread (any large textile can work)

Welt cording, about 5 yards (will depend on the size of your chair)

Seam allowance is ½ inch, unless otherwise noted.

DO

1 Lay the textile over the chair, letting it conform to the chair's shape. Cut about ½ inch beyond the edge of the chair along both sides. Cut 2 inches beyond the chair's bottom edge at the front and the back, as shown.

2 Use the leftover portion of the textile to cut the side pieces. Lay the chair on its side to make this step easier. Place the textile over the chair's side area and, in the same manner as in step 1, cut ½ inch beyond the edge of the chair's side perimeter. Cut 2 inches beyond the bottom edge, as shown. Use this piece as a pattern to cut the second side piece. (Make sure to reverse it so that you cut the mirror image of it.)

3 Make the cording (see page 126 for directions). Using a zipper foot, stitch the cording to the right side of the seat section along the two side edges, as shown.

4 Pin the two side pieces to the seat section with right sides facing. Use the zipper foot to sew the pieces together, stitching as close to the cording as possible.

5 Pull about 1 inch of cording from its sheath at each end and snip off, as shown, to reduce bulk and make hemming easier.

6 Stitch a 1-inch double-fold hem along the entire bottom edge of the slipcover.

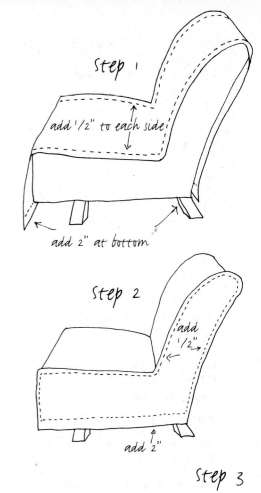

step 1

add ½" to each side

add 2" at bottom

step 2

add ½"

add 2"

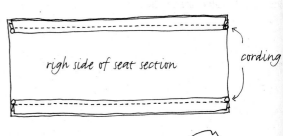

step 3

righ side of seat section

cording

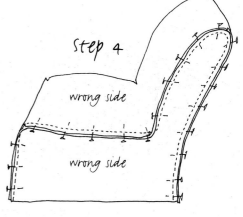

step 4

wrong side

wrong side

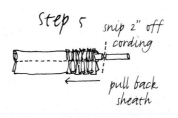

step 5

snip 2" off cording

pull back sheath

obi placemats

SEE P 68

GET

Tool kit (page 123)

Serger (optional)

2 obis of varying widths (and pleasing pattern/color combination)

Seam allowance is ½ inch, unless otherwise noted.

note

Placemats vary in size. The dimensions called out in these instructions are within a standard range, but feel free to adjust them to suit your needs.

DO

1 Cut both obis to the same length (approximately 19 inches). Cut the narrower obi in half lengthwise, as shown. Finish the cut edges with a zigzag stitch or serger.

2 Pin the two halves of the cut obi to the underside of the finished edges of the wide obi, as shown, making sure that there is at least ¼ inch of overlap. Topstitch ⅛ inch from the inside edges of the center obi. If the lengths vary a bit, trim them to the same length.

3 Stitch a ½-inch double-fold hem on each side of the placemat. If your obis are too bulky for a double-fold hem, a single fold will do, as long as you serge or zigzag the raw edges first.

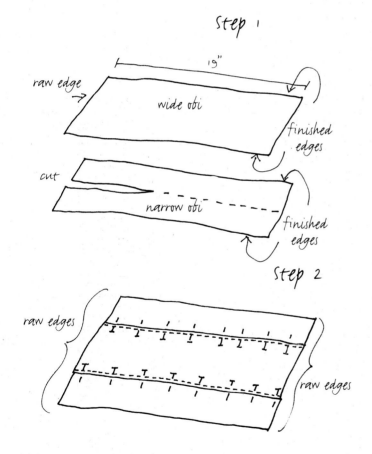

Step 1

raw edge

19"

wide obi

finished edges

cut

narrow obi

finished edges

Step 2

raw edges

raw edges

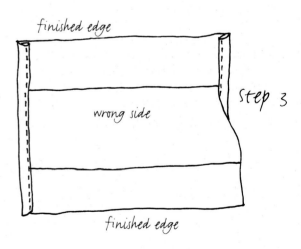

Step 3

finished edge

wrong side

finished edge

another idea

Cut the obies to a much longer length for a stunning table runner.

scarf-painted cabinet

SEE P 69

GET

Drop cloth

Masking tape

2-inch flat brush

Utility knife

Old towel (for sticky hands)

White painted metal or wood cabinet

3 to 5 large lightweight scarves (for best results use silk or chiffon with simple geometric patterns)

Matte-finish decoupage medium (also called glue), 16 ounces

Acrylic sealer (optional)

DO

1 Make sure the cabinet is clean and dust-free. Position the cabinet on the drop cloth, and begin with the door closed and latched.

2 Experiment with composition by taping the scarves to the cabinet. (Don't worry if they're not the perfect size; you can fill in the gaps later with fragments of additional scarves.) When you arrive at your design, take a picture or make a rough sketch to help you remember it, then remove the scarves.

3 Re-tape the top scarf into place, this time pulling it taut in each direction (across the front, over the door, and back along each side). Cut out a small section of the scarf to accommodate the latch. Secure the scarf with enough tape to prevent it from shifting as you apply the glue.

4 Dip the brush into the glue as if it was paint, and apply it to the scarf. Begin at the center front and radiate out toward the edges. Keep smoothing with the brush and your fingers to work out any bubbles or wrinkles, until the scarf is completely covered with glue. (Remove the tape as you approach the edges.) This can get a little messy, but don't worry about perfection. The glue will be clear when dry.

5 Before the glue dries completely, use the utility knife to cut the scarf along the perimeter of the door to free it for opening. Open the door, then use the brush to smooth out the raw edges and make sure they lie flat.

6 Repeat this process with each scarf until the surface of the cabinet is covered to your liking. Use scissors to cut any overhang at bottom and back edges, then brush edges flat.

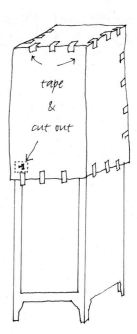

tape & cut out

step 3

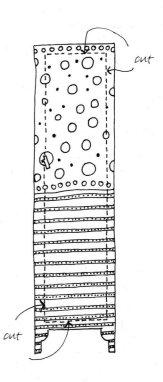

cut

cut

step 5

7 Once the glue is completely dry, apply a clear acrylic sealer for durability, if you'd like.

pleated drapery pillow sham

GET

Tool kit (page 123)

1 pleated drapery panel, at least 21 inches wide at the pleated top edge and 64 inches long (for a standard size sham)

Seam allowance is ½ inch, unless otherwise noted.

DO

1 Measure and cut a 30½-inch length from the panel, measuring from the top pleated edge. If the panel is lined, cut the lining off at the base of the pleats.

2 Lay this section of drapery flat by fanning out the unpleated area. Mark and cut a 21 x 30½-inch rectangle, as shown.

3 From the remainder of the drapery, cut a 21 x 31½-inch rectangle. Turn one end under, twice, and stitch a 1-inch double-fold hem, as shown.

4 With right sides facing, pin the two pieces together. Stitch the sides and the unfinished end, pivoting at the corners. Clip the bottom corners, turn the sham right side out, and press the seams.

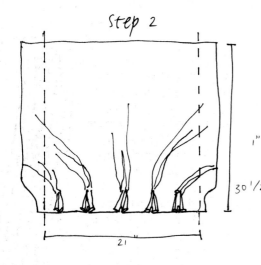

step 2

30 ½"

21"

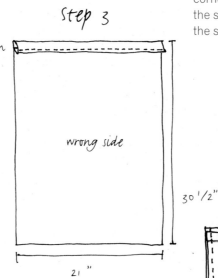

step 3

1" hem

wrong side

30 ½"

21"

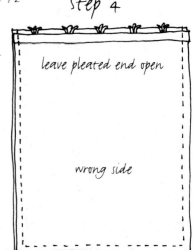

step 4

leave pleated end open

wrong side

note

This sham remains open at the side like a traditional pillowcase. If you want your sham to have a closed end, stitch a few lengths of hook-and-loop tape to the inside edge of the front (between the pleats) and to the inside edge of the back, where necessary.

damask drapery coverlet

GET

Tool kit (page 123)

3 vintage damask drapery panels, at least 94 inches long

Seam allowance is ½ inch, unless otherwise noted.

note

Most people assume that a vintage drapery panel would be "dry clean only." I have no tolerance for prima donna fabrics that need to be coddled. I throw everything into the washing machine, and if it doesn't come out intact, then I didn't want to use it anyway. Damask is totally machine-washable. It may shrink a little—so wash **before** you cut—but it becomes softer, more lustrous, and silky.

DO

1 Cut all three panels to the same length. The panels shown here are 92 inches long (finished length). If you prefer a coverlet that provides greater coverage (extends to the floor), measure the height of the bed and adjust to the desired length. Add 2 inches to the measurement to allow for a 1-inch hem at each end.

2 Measure the bed to determine the desired width of the coverlet, and combine the three panels to meet this measurement. Make the panels three different widths for added interest. Add 1 inch to the width of the center panel and 1 to ½ inch to the outside panels to allow for seam allowances and hem.

3 With right sides facing, stitch the panels together, one at a time.

4 Press the seam allowances to one side, and topstitch in place. Turn edges under to make a 1-inch double-fold hem on all sides, as shown.

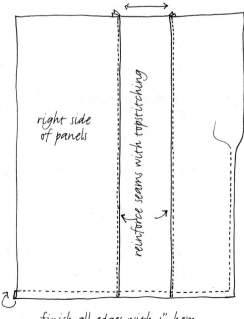

right side of panels

reinforce seams with topstitching

finish all edges with 1" hem

zipper tapestry

SEE P **71**

GET

Tool kit (page 123)

Metal zippers, any shape or size, and as many as you can find (If you use nylon zippers, you will not achieve the same effect at all, so no substitutions!)

DO

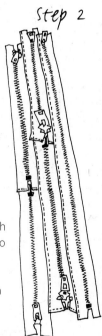

step 2

1 Begin by sewing a few zippers together, end to end, until you reach the desired length. Repeat this process until you have a number of zipper strands of approximately equal length.

2 Sew the zipper strands together lengthwise by overlapping them about ¼ inch and topstitching through both layers. The ends don't have to be even.

3 Keep going until you reach the intended size.

GET

Tool kit (page 123)

Salvaged zippers, size of your choice

Wool scraps, longer than the length of the zippers

Seam allowance is ½ inch, unless otherwise noted.

DO

1 Cut the wool scraps into rectangles. You can make these pouches any size you want, depending on the length of the zippers, of course. The short end of the rectangle must be equal to or less than the length of the zipper. For a guideline, the pouches shown were made from pieces measuring approximately 7 x 9 inches, 10 x 15 inches, and 12 x 16 inches.

2 Topstitch the zipper to the right side of the short ends of the rectangle. This is much easier to accomplish if the zipper is in the open position.

3 Close the zipper and turn the fabric wrong side out. Lay it flat, positioning the top of the zipper about 1 inch from the folded edge. Pin the sides together. Before you stitch, open the zipper partway, to make it easier to turn the pouch right side out later. Stitch each side edge. Trim the top corners to reduce bulk.

To make a looped handle from the zipper, let the zipper extend beyond the right edge of the pouch. When stitching that seam, don't stitch across the zipper, but just up to its edge, and then backstitch. Resume stitching on the other side of the zipper, again with a backstitch. When you turn the pouch right-side out, you can pull the zipper through this gap. Make a loop with the zipper, and tuck and pin its end back inside the gap in the seam. Now you can hand-stitch across the zipper to close the gap.

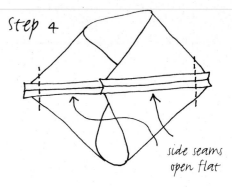

step 4

side seams open flat

4 Lay the bottom corners flat, and stitch a gusset about 1 inch from the tip of the corner and perpendicular to the side seams. Trim off the excess. Open the zipper and turn the pouch right side out.

zippered obi variation

Make these pouches the same way as the others. The only difference is embellishment: After topstitching the zipper in place (step 2), pin some trim along the edge of each side of the zipper, and topstitch. The trim can be anything that strikes your fancy, maybe something from your remnant stash.

By the way, some obis are two layers of fabric lined with interfacing. To reduce bulk, you may want to separate the layers and use only the top layer for this project.

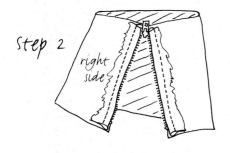

step 2

right side

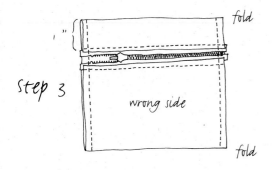

step 3

fold

wrong side

fold

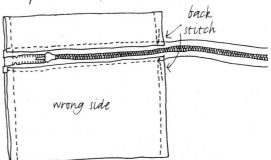

step 3 (for looped-handle version)

back stitch

wrong side

trampoline window treatment

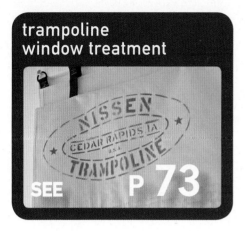

SEE P 73

GET

Tool kit (page 123)

Industrial sewing machine

Screws and screwdriver, if you opt for hooks

1 trampoline canvas, straps and hardware intact

Double-fold seam binding, 1-inch wide, enough for both sides of the window treatment

Nylon upholstery thread, matching color

Nails with decorative heads, or metal hooks

note

If an industrial machine is not available to you, it's possible that an ordinary sewing machine will work. Be sure to use a heavy-duty needle, and stitch very slowly.

DO

1 Plan for a finished edge of the trampoline (with straps and hardware) to be the bottom edge of the window covering. Get the inside measurements of the window and plot them out on the canvas, using a yardstick and fabric chalk. For interest, plan around a printed graphic area—be sure to position it in the bottom third so it will show when the curtain is raised. Add 2 inches to the vertical measurement at the top. Do not add to the width measurement. Cut out the rectangle.

2 Cover the raw edges on both sides by applying seam binding.

3 Pin and stitch a 1-inch double-fold hem at the top of the canvas piece.

4 From another area of the trampoline, cut off the same number of D-ring straps that hang from the bottom of the canvas piece. Cut these straps to the desired length, and pin the cut ends to the underside at the top of the canvas. Line them up directly across from the straps at the bottom edge. Stitch in place.

5 Cut two more D-ring straps, and position them on the canvas one third of the distance from the bottom edge. Place them in line with the second straps from each edge at the top and bottom and attach securely using upholstery thread. These straps provide a way to lift the shade.

6 Measure the distance between the straps to determine where to place the decorative nails or hooks into the wall for hanging. Pound in the nails or attach the hooks, then hang the trampoline.

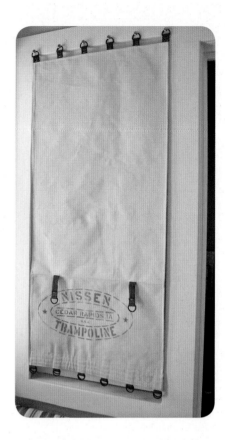

buckled-up headboard

SEE P 74

GET

Tool kit (page 123)

Electric knife (cuts through foam like butter)

Spray adhesive

7-inch upholstery needle

Bed headboard that's due for an update

Medium density foam, 2 inches thick, the size of the headboard to be covered

High-loft 100 percent polyester batting, the size of the headboard to be covered

Duct tape

Linen, medium to heavyweight: see steps 3 and 9 to determine how much you need

Cheaper utilitarian fabric for the headboard back (optional)

7 belt buckles (or large buttons for a more traditional look)

7 small plain buttons

Waxed string

Seam allowance is ½ inch, unless otherwise noted.

note

Material amounts will vary depending on the size of the headboard.

DO

1 Measure the length and width of the headboard, and use the electric knife to cut the foam to those dimensions. (The fabric store will cut foam to length, but you're usually on your own to cut the width.) Also cut the batting to this size.

2 Attach the foam to the front of the headboard with duct tape (yes, I said duct tape). Wrap the tape around the backside of the headboard, as shown, to make sure it is secure. Following manufacturer's instructions, apply spray adhesive to one side of the foam, and attach the batting.

3 Cut two pieces of linen fabric 1 inch larger than the width of the headboard and 3 inches more than the height. Or, since the back of the headboard is usually not visible, you can use cheaper fabric for that side. In that case, cut one piece of linen and then cut a piece of the other fabric to the same size.

4 With the right sides facing, stitch the pieces together at the sides and the top. Make a 1-inch gusset at the two top corners, as shown. Stitch a ¾-inch double-fold hem along the bottom edge.

5 Turn the cover right-sides out and slip it over the padded headboard. It should fit very snugly.

6 Use the measuring tape to determine the placement of the buckles (or buttons). There are no rules here, but you may want them to be equidistant. Mark the spots with pins.

7 Cut a 24-inch length of waxed string for every buckle or button. Loop the string through the center bar of the buckle (or shank of the button), and thread both ends through the eye of the upholstery needle. Push the needle straight through the padding to the backside, as shown, and release the string from the needle. You will have two lengths of string hanging at the back. Repeat this process until all the buckles or buttons are placed where you want them.

8 Thread the two lengths of string hanging from the backside through two different holes in a small button. As in the first step of tying a shoe, cross one string over and under the other, as shown, and pull toward the headboard. The button will prevent the string from pulling through the fabric. As the string pulls the button toward the back of the headboard, the buckle (or button) on the front side will make an indentation in the foam. When you achieve the right amount of indentation, make a double knot in the string. Repeat this process with the remaining buckles, pulling them all to an even depth.

9 If you have a footboard, cover it (without padding) by following steps 3 through 5 with one slight change: The slipcover will need to be shorter on the inside of the footboard to accommodate the side rails, while the outside remains long enough to cover the full face of it. (Also, both sides of the footboard are visible so you can't cheat with diffrent fabric on one side.) For easier hemming, you may want to stitch the double-fold hem for the back before stitching it to the front piece.

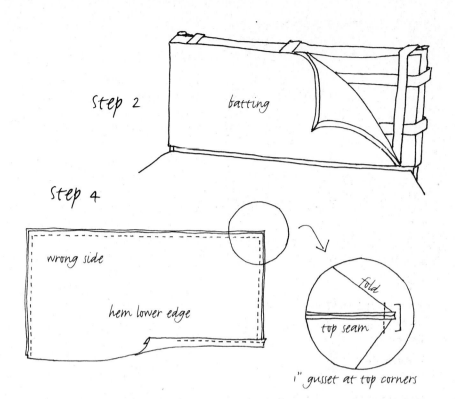

step 2

batting

step 4

wrong side

hem lower edge

fold

top seam

1" gusset at top corners

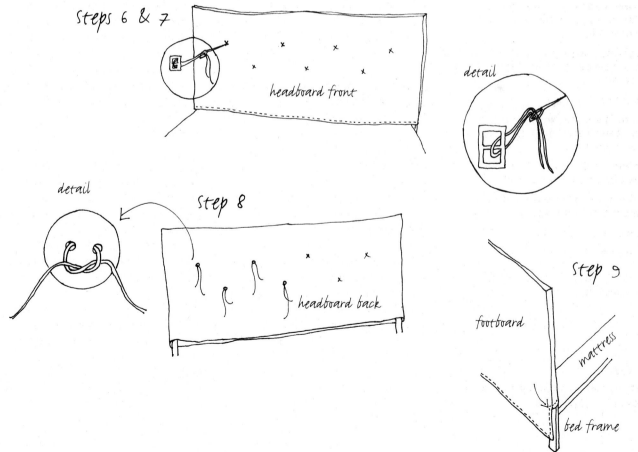

steps 6 & 7

headboard front

detail

detail

step 8

headboard back

step 9

footboard

mattress

bed frame

vinyl revival

SEE P 75

GET

Tool kit (page 123)

Wide-mouth container

Paintbrush, 2-inch

Injured vinyl furniture of your choice

Duct tape

Upholstery or drapery fabric with rubberized backing (necessary for optimum adhesion)

Decoupage medium or bookbinder's glue (any water-based adhesive that remains flexible when dry)

DO

1 Bandage the injured area with duct tape.

2 Determine the size of the area you wish to cover and cut the fabric to fit. The best solution, visually, is to cover the entire section where the damage is located:

• Choose a logical border, such as the piping in the seams, to end the "patch."

• If you are repairing a loose cushion, the piping will follow the entire perimeter, so simply cut the fabric to fit the area inside the piping.

• If you are repairing an attached seat or back (as shown here) add about 4 inches to tuck into the crevice of the sofa or chair.

3 Tuck the fabric snugly into the crevice and smooth it out, making sure the edges line up properly with the piping. Lift and pin the fabric away from the area to be glued.

4 Pour the glue into a wide-mouth container that will accommodate the brush. Apply the glue evenly over the entire vinyl surface, leaving a 1-inch border along the piping. Lay the fabric over the glue and smooth it out flat, starting from the center back and working toward the sides and front. Recheck the edges at this point, as you may have to do some more trimming if the fabric has shifted or stretched a bit. Now you can continue gluing to the edge of the piping. Make sure you get good coverage to insure strong adhesion along the edges.

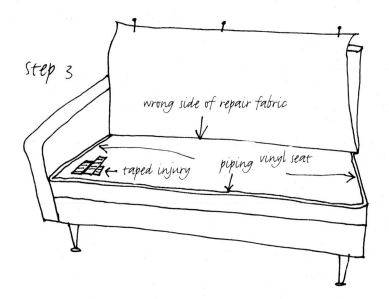

step 3

wrong side of repair fabric

← taped injury   piping vinyl seat

5 Apply glue to the top side of the fabric along the raw edges to prevent fraying.

Allow three to four hours drying time.

step 5

apply glue to top side of fabric at perimeter

resurfaced table

SEE P **76**

GET

Tool kit (page 123)

Staple gun and staples

Paintbrush

Clear polyurethane with satin finish, 1 quart

Table with a great base, but a not-so-great top

Enough fabric to wrap the surface

DO

Before you start

When considering fabric for this project, keep in mind that the polyurethane will alter the colors. If you like how the fabric looks when it's wet, you have a winner.

1 Cut the fabric large enough to wrap the surface and sides of the tabletop(s), with a couple of extra inches to staple to the underside.

2 Lay the table upside down over the fabric. Pull the fabric over one side, and staple it at the midpoint to the underside of the table. Pull fabric taut, and staple it to the opposite side, as shown. Repeat this procedure in the opposite direction, then start adding staples from each center toward the corners.

3 Continue working in this manner, from the center of each side toward the corners. Fold the fabric at the corners as you would when wrapping a gift box.

4 Turn the table right side up. Use the paintbrush to apply a generous coat of polyurethane to the top and sides, until you reach saturation point. Let it dry 24 hours (or per manufacturer's directions) before you apply a second coat.

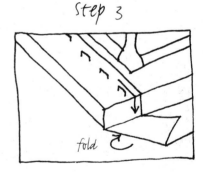

step 2

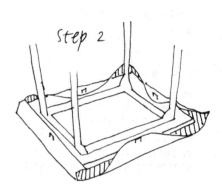

step 3

fold

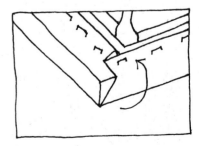

mid-century tie chair

SEE P77

GET

Tool kit (page 123)

Small flat-head screwdriver for lifting staples and tacks (You may need a second screwdriver depending on the type of screws you will be removing.)

Needle-nose pliers

Staple gun and staples

Small hammer

Side chair worthy of rescue (with removable back)

Remnant for tie backing, 3 inches larger than the chair back (any medium-weight scrap will do, because it won't be visible)

Vintage ties, 8 to 12, depending on width (which varies by decade)

Thread (don't worry about it matching perfectly everywhere; the contrast adds interest)

Coordinating remnant, 1 inch larger than the dimensions of the chair back

Decorative furniture nails, 30 to 40 nails (I chose smooth-head, nickel-plated nails to coordinate with the chair's chrome frame.)

Seam allowance is ½ inch, unless otherwise noted.

DO

1 Remove the fabric from the outside back of the chair (set it aside to refer to later). This will reveal the screws that attach the back to the frame. Remove the screws, and take my advice—keep them together in a safe place and remember where that safe place is. It's also a good idea to mark the back's top edge to help you remember the correct position when it comes time to reattach it to the frame. (The chair I used also had wooden arms, which I removed and later reattached when the transformation was complete.)

2 Now that you've freed the seat back, you can move to a comfortable work surface and remove the fabric from the front side. Use the small flat-head screwdriver and needle-nose pliers to lift the tacks or staples from the wood. Dispose of all tacks carefully and immediately (spouses and children dislike stepping on them). Once it's removed, use the old fabric to determine the size of the new backing material onto which you will sew the ties. Cut the backing piece and lay it horizontally on your work surface.

3 Now the fun part! Pull out your stash of vintage ties, and lay them vertically across the backing in alternating directions. (Note that you can cut the ties in half and use both ends.) Do this until you reach a pleasing combination of colors and patterns. (This can take anywhere from five minutes to five hours, if you're anything like me.) Take a picture of your layout or number your ties on the back, to help you remember their positioning.

note

No need to spend money on special upholstery tools. You can tackle this project with very rudimentary household tools. I don't use anything fancy, and I do this a lot.

step 4

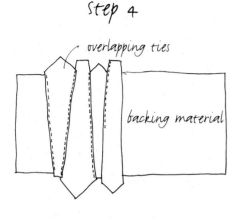

overlapping ties

backing material

step 5

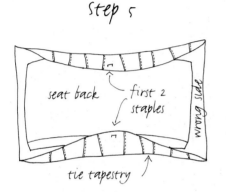

seat back

first 2 staples

wrong side

tie tapestry

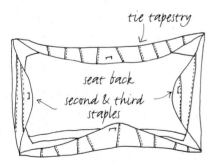

tie tapestry

seat back

second & third staples

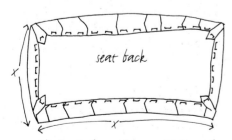

seat back

x

x

x

Work from the center towards each corner. staple the corners last.

4 Remove the ties from the backing. To avoid getting poked by numerous pins as you sew, start by pinning just two or three ties at a time to the backing material and stitching them in place. I usually start from the left side and work my way across. Make sure the ties overlap by about $\frac{1}{4}$ inch to avoid any gaps, and use lots of pins. Stitch as close as you can to the edge of any ties that lie on top, to make sure that you are also catching the edge of the underlying tie. Keep pinning and stitching in this manner until you've completely covered the backing material. Cut the ties to the same width of the backing. Press your fabulous new "tie tapestry" with a cool iron.

5 The next step is to stretch the tie tapestry over the seat back:

• Place the tapestry, right side down, on your work surface. Place the seat back, front side down, over it.

• Pull the tapestry over the top of the seat and place the first staple at the center back approximately $\frac{1}{2}$ inch from the edge of the seat back. Snug up the tapestry around the bottom of the seat back, and place the second staple at the lower center back, again, about $\frac{1}{2}$ inch from the edge of the seat back.

• Repeat this procedure in the opposite direction (right to left, as shown), and pull the tapestry taut before you staple.

• Continue working in this manner, from the center of each side toward the corners, until you have secured the tapestry on all sides with staples measuring about 1 inch apart. Fold and staple the corners last, as shown. Whew! Admire your work.

6 Retrieve the screws you removed earlier from their secure (remember?) location. Reattach the seat back to its original position on the frame.

7 Measure the fabric that you removed from the outside, back in step 1. Cut the coordinating remnant to these dimensions. Turn the edges under and pin them to the seat back, pulling taut as you go. Be careful not to leave the underlying staples exposed.

8 For a nailhead trim (see page 126), use the small hammer and decorative furniture nails to tack the fabric at each corner, removing the pins as you go. Place the next nails at the center top and center bottom, then repeat at center right and left, as shown. Use as many nails as you wish to finish the job. You may choose to place the nails edge to edge, or measure a distance anywhere from $\frac{1}{2}$ inch to 2 inches between the nails. Just be consistent and mark the measurements before you pound.

step 8

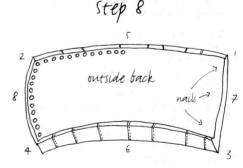

5

2

1

outside back

8

nails

7

4

6

3

Place corner nails first, then center top and bottom, and then center right and left. Continue filling in the areas between the nails.

happy hanky stool

SEE P 78

GET

Tool kit (page 123)

Fabric chalk

Upholstery tacks

Small round footstool

Unbleached cotton canvas, 1 yard

Welt cording, enough to encircle the top of the stool (optional)

2 printed handkerchiefs

Pattern tissue

Twill tape, about 2 yards, depending on the size of the footstool

Seam allowance is ½ inch, unless otherwise noted.

note

The tissue paper skirt makes this project a little bit arty and a little bit fragile. Not recommended for households with pets or small children.

DO

1 Lay the footstool upside down on the wrong side of the canvas. With fabric chalk, trace the shape of the stool onto the canvas. Cut ¾ inch outside of this line.

2 If you want cording, make it now (see page 126 for directions). If you don't want cording, skip to step 3. Pin the finished cording to the perimeter of the round top piece as shown. Stitch it in place, starting about 3 inches from the end of the cording to leave room to splice it at the other end. Use the zipper foot, with the needle set to the outside of the foot. Keep raw edges aligned, and stitch as close to the cording as you can. Finish the ends, as shown.

3 Measure the circumference of the stool and the width of the side. Add 1 inch to each dimension, and cut the canvas to this size to create the side piece.

4 With wrong sides facing, fold the side piece in half and stitch the raw ends together, as shown.

5 With right sides facing, stitch the side piece to the top piece as shown, again stitching as close to the cording as possible. Turn ½ inch of the bottom edge toward the inside, and press flat.

6 Fold the two handkerchiefs into fourths, and cut along the folds to create four equal squares per hanky. Cut each of these squares in half at a diagonal to create eight triangular pieces per hanky. Discard the triangles with three raw edges or save for another project. You will use only the triangles with two finished edges and one cut edge.

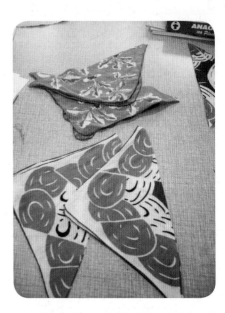

7 Overlap the hankies as you pin the raw edges, as shown, to the underside of the folded and pressed edge of the side piece. You may have to fiddle with this until you get equal lengths of overlap all around. Topstitch the hankies to the bottom of the side piece. You have finished the footstool's "cap"—but don't put it on the stool yet.

8 To make the tissue skirt, collect some old pattern pieces you will no longer need—the larger the better. Cut two lengths of twill tape about 6 inches longer than the perimeter of the footstool. Gather or scrunch the tissue pieces into vertical pleats, and sandwich the top edges between the two lengths of twill tape, pinning in place as you do so. When you reach the end of one piece of tissue, simply overlap the next piece and keep pinning until you have enough length to reach around the footstool's perimeter. Now stitch the tissue to the twill tape along the entire length.

9 With the upholstery tacks, attach the skirt to the side of the footstool by tacking through the twill tape about every 3 or 4 inches. Don't worry about the length of the tissue skirt until you've tacked it in place. You can cut it to the desired length when you're finished.

10 Place the hanky trimmed "cap" over the tissue skirt, and keep it away from your cats!

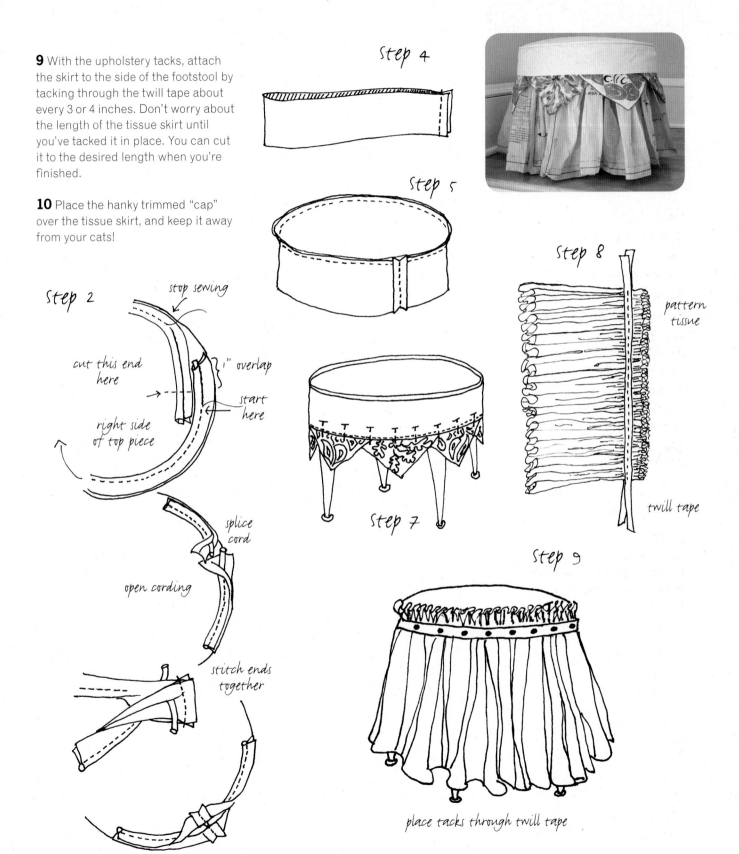

step 4

step 5

step 8

pattern tissue

twill tape

Step 2

stop sewing

cut this end here

1" overlap

start here

right side of top piece

splice cord

open cording

stitch ends together

step 7

step 9

place tacks through twill tape

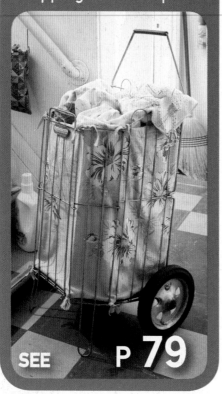

SEE P **79**

GET

Tool kit (page 123)

Metal utility cart

Vintage fabric, 1½ yards

Twill tape, ribbon, or seam binding, 3 yards

Seam allowance is ½ inch, unless otherwise noted.

DO

1 Use the removable base of the cart as a pattern to create the bottom of the liner. Use fabric chalk to trace this shape onto the wrong side of the lining fabric, as shown. Add ½ inch for seam allowance before cutting out the shape. (If your cart doesn't have a removable base, simply trace the bottom of the cart itself onto a piece of paper.)

2 To determine the dimensions of the side of the liner, measure the perimeter of the bottom of the liner (step 1) and add 1 inch. Measure the height of the cart on the inside, from the floor to the highest point, and add 3 inches. The perimeter of the bottom piece for the cart shown measured 52 inches, and the inside height measured 25 inches, so the cut size for this liner was 53 x 28 inches. Yours may be slightly different. Fold this rectangle in half with the right sides together, and pin. Stitch a seam along the vertical measurements.

3 Cut twelve 9-inch lengths of twill tape. Fold six of them in half, and pin them to the right side of the liner bottom at each corner, as shown. The folded edge of the tape should align with the cut edge of the liner bottom. Machine-baste the tabs into place.

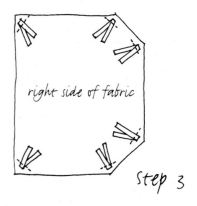

step 1

base of cart cut '/2" larger

liner fabric wrong side

right side of fabric

step 3

4 With right sides facing, pin the bottom edge of the liner sides to the perimeter of the liner bottom. (For a clean look, align the side seam with one of the back corners.) The twill tabs will be sandwiched between the two layers. Stitch ½ inch from the edge. Trim the corners and seam allowance, then turn the liner right side out and place it inside the cart to check the fit.

5 To fit the liner to the cart:

• Fold and pin the top edge of the liner toward the inside, so that the folded edge lines up with the top edge of the cart. Most carts are lower in the front than in the back. Adjust for this by making a deeper fold in the front, and fold the sides at a diagonal to follow the slant.

- Remove the liner from the cart.

- Trim the raw edge at the top to an even 3 inches all the way around. Tuck the raw edge under about ½ inch, and then fold under again. Stitch the 2½-inch hem along the top edge.

- Fold the remaining twill tape pieces in half and pin to the top edge at each corner, as shown.

- Secure the twill tabs with a few stitches back and forth across each one.

- Press the hem and seams flat.

6 Place the liner in the cart. Attach the liner to the top and bottom by tying the twill tabs to the cart at each corner.

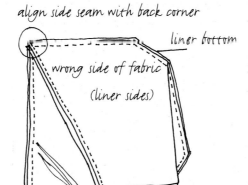

align side seam with back corner

liner bottom

wrong side of fabric
(liner sides)

step 4

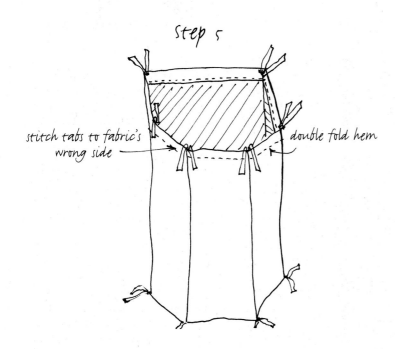

step 5

stitch tabs to fabric's wrong side

double fold hem

tools and techniques

I usually get by with ordinary tools. And the techniques I use are also simple and may be a bit unorthodox, as I am self-taught.

Basically, I get by with ordinary everyday tools. I don't believe in spending a fortune on fancy gadgets and power tools because they usually break or make too much noise or, inevitably, get lost. I scrounge for used tools as much as I scrounge for materials. I enjoy working "unplugged" to keep it simple, and I will admit than I am a bit of a Luddite. Of course, I use electric sewing machines, but they're nothing flashy. Most of my time is spent behind my trusty Singer made in the 1950s that I purchased on the cheap at a garage sale, cabinet included. It only has a straight stitch but it will sew through almost anything, and it just keeps on ticking. I use the overcast stitch of a serger when I want to finish raw edges, and an industrial machine, also purchased used, for the occasional heavy-duty work.

As for upholstery tools, I do own a power staple gun but it is not as powerful as it claims to be. Maybe someday I'll invest in a better one, but for now I'm content with my little hammer and cut tacks. When rehabbing furniture, I use a needle-nose pliers and a small flathead screwdriver to remove old tacks and staples.

Techniques I use are also simple and some may be a bit unorthodox since, for the most part, I am self-taught. I do I have a few tips to pass on, as I've been working in this manner for a long time, but honestly, as far as special tricks-of-the-trade—there aren't that many. The technique I am stellar at is covering up mistakes!

Workroom Staples
Sewing Machine and Tool Kit

The most important tool in my studio is, obviously, my sewing machine, which is necessary for making most of these projects. I like to have many different colors of thread on hand and within reach. This also goes for pre-wound bobbins and a zipper foot. A zigzag stitch is very nice to have for finishing seams and to prevent fraying, but I generally stick with a basic straight stitch. Since I sell my work, I feel it needs to look professional on the inside as well as outside. So I use a serger to finish seams and raw edges. A range of needle sizes to meet a broad range of potential materials is required when you move from a fragile silk scarf one day to a trampoline canvas the next. I go through needles like some people go through paper clips. In addition to your sewing machine(s), then, at the right is a list of commonly used sewing staples to keep within reach while making the projects in this book.

basic tool kit

- Sewing machine
- Zipper foot
- Needles (hand and machine)
- Thread
- Scissors
- Hammer
- Pins
- Measuring tools
- Fabric chalk and marking tools
- Seam ripper
- Iron and ironing board

Needles

Embroidery (large eyed), curved, and extra-long upholstery needles make many jobs easier, and some projects are impossible without them. For instance, you will definitely need a 7-inch (or longer) needle when piercing foam to make a buttoned cushion.

Cutting tools

I have sort of a rotational system with scissors. I try to use my high-end dressmaking shears exclusively for light to medium-weight fabrics, but beyond that I use inexpensive scissors. The brand new sharp pair is assigned to all types of heavier textiles, trims, and other soft goods until it begins to dull, and then it becomes the paper scissors for a spell, until it finally becomes the junk scissors for anything and everything. When you use this method it's a good idea to label each scissors to identify what stage of life it's currently in.

The electric knife that formerly belonged to my mother has not touched a roast turkey since it's been in my possession. As a foam cutter, it can't be beat.

Measuring instruments

It's helpful to own an extra long (60-inch) metal straightedge for marking off large areas, but it's not necessary. A yardstick or a measuring tape is usually adequate. A right-angle triangle is very useful since the majority of shapes cut in this type of work are rectilinear.

Zippers

Cushion covers usually require very long zippers. It's usually possible to remove zippers from the upholstered items you are replacing and reuse them in your new creation. A clever trick I learned from a friend is to take two zippers and install them with their

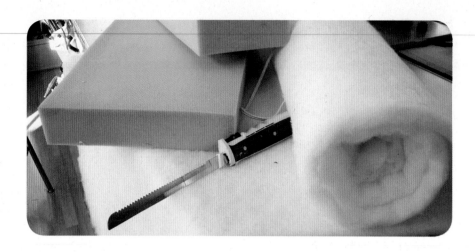

tops (open ends) facing each other to create a large opening. "Endless" zipper can also be purchased, which is one long continuous length of zipper on a roll sold with numerous zipper pulls, which can be cut to any desired length.

Cording

Welt cording, usually made from cotton or paper tissue, is necessary for making your own cording. Since I use it extensively, I buy it in large wheels from upholstery suppliers, but fabric stores have smaller quantities. It comes in different diameters, but the larger size is extremely difficult to use with a regular home sewing machine. Instructions for making and attaching cording are on page 126.

Foam and polyester batting

Decent quality all-purpose foam can be found at most large fabric/craft stores in a range of thicknesses, but you'll need to visit an upholstery supply store if you're looking for a variety of densities (soft, firm, extra firm). A full sheet of foam measures about 24 x 90 inches and is sold by the inch. Polyester batting, also available at fabric stores, is similar to (but a little tougher) than quilt batting. Batting can be applied to the surface of foam to give it a softer look and feel and to

help round out the edges, as in the Buckled-Up Headboard on page 112. Foam has a stickiness about it, which makes it difficult to slip into a tightly fitting cover; the batting will aid in that process.

Adhesives

An all-purpose spray adhesive is the best way to adhere batting to foam because it will prevent shifting of the product. It also works well when joining pieces of foam, which is sometimes necessary when making large or oddly shaped cushions or when you want to make use of smaller-sized leftovers.

Staple gun, staples, upholstery hammer, and tacks

I've already mentioned my lame staple gun. Do as I say and not as I do...if you see many upholstery projects in your future, invest in a decent power staple gun to avoid frustration! An upholstery hammer with a small tapered head and cut tacks (available at any hardware store) or a manual staple gun will suffice if you plan on just being a dabbler.

Special Techniques

If you're attempting these projects I'll assume you possess some fundamental sewing and crafting skills. Some of the upholstery-type projects may be new to you, so here are a few tips to help pave the way. I've also included my scarf-painting technique for fun!

Scarf "Painting"

Essentially, this process is simply gluing a sheer, silk, or otherwise lightweight scarf to any surface. It's really just a modified version of "decoupage," which was all the rage back in the 1970s (using mostly paper items). Gluing fabric is a little trickier than paper because of its flexibility and tendency to wrinkle and move under the brush. I typically apply the decoupage medium to the surface first and then place the scarf in the desired spot. I then dip the brush into the medium again and apply it to the surface of the scarf, brushing from the center out to smooth the wrinkles.

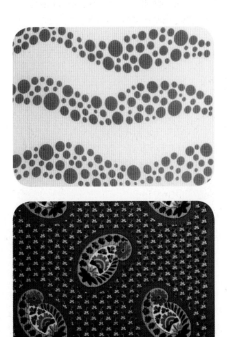

Make a Pillow Flange

A flange is simply a "floppy" border around a pillow that extends beyond the stuffed area. Flanges can be of any desired width as long as you incorporate the width into the calculations for your cutting dimensions. If you want a 1-inch flange, you will need to add 1 inch to the size of the pillow form you are covering, in addition to the ½ inch for seam allowances, to get your cutting dimensions. (Add 2 inches for a 2-inch flange and so on.)

1 Assemble your pillow cover as you would an ordinary style cover.

2 Turn right side out, and press seams flat.

3 Pin the pillow front to the pillow back around its perimeter (about 1 inch from the edge for a 1-inch flange, and so on) to prevent shifting.

4 With the front of the pillow facing up, topstitch around the entire perimeter at the desired distance from the edge.

variation

To add texture to a flange, repeat step 4 at a decreasing distance from the edge, creating many rows of equidistant topstitching.

topstitch to form flange

Make a Double-fold Hem

To make a double-fold hem, simply fold the raw edge of your fabric over about ½ inch and then again as you feed it through the machine so that you are stitching along a folded edge. Essentially you are just tucking the raw edge under as you stitch. This type of hem is appropriate for fine- and medium-weave fabrics, but may add too much bulk with heavier fabrics.

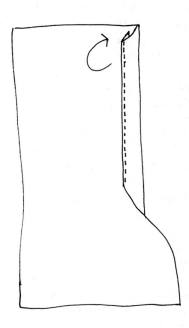

Make Cording

1 Cut the fabric on the bias (45° angle to the selvage) into 2-inch strips, as shown.

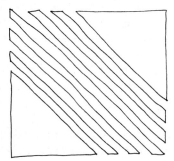

2 With right sides facing, stitch the strips together end to end. Align the selvage edges to make a "V" shape, as shown, and stitch along the grain line.

3 With the needle set to the left side of the zipper foot, wrap the fabric around the cord as you feed it through the machine. Stitch as close to the cord as possible. Since the fabric is cut on the bias, pulling it toward you slightly as you sew will cause it to stretch a bit, giving it a tighter fit. When you reach a seam in the fabric strip, flatten the seam allowance open as you stitch over the seam.

4 Individual project instructions will tell you how to attach the cording; generally, you start and stop stitching the cording several inches into the strip so you can encase the ends of the cording before you finish sewing it to your project. To do so, open the seams of the cording a few inches on both ends. With right sides facing, stitch the ends together in a ½-inch seam.

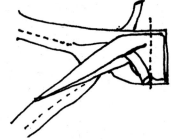

5 Open the seam and lay the two ends of bare cord side by side. Trim away the excess and splice. Wrap the fabric strip around the cording once again, and finish stitching the cording to the project.

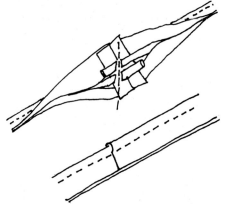

Add Nail Head Trim

When applying a nail-head detail to a piece of furniture, as in the Sanctuary Chair on page 82, secure the fabric first with enough ordinary tacks or staples to keep it properly in place. Follow up with the decorative tacks, removing the temporary placement tacks as you are able. To keep the decorative nails equidistant, cut a strip of cardboard or other stiff material to the desired distance and use it as a marker.

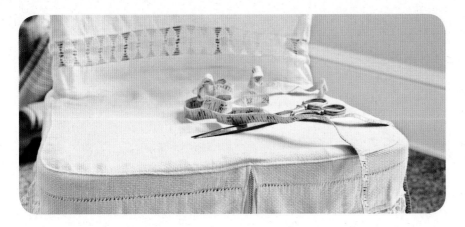

Make Slipcovers

Making a slipcover is not as difficult as you might think. Approach it like a three-dimensional puzzle. Study the piece of furniture and break it down in your mind as to how many pieces the puzzle will have and what their shapes will be (which will determine where your seams should fall) before you start cutting, and use remnants or inexpensive muslin for the pattern. If your chair is symmetrical you can treat it as you would a dress form, pinning your pieces together with right sides facing, following its contours and then cutting at least ½ inch beyond the pins to include seam allowances. Baste the pieces together section by section, turn right-side out, try it on to check the fit, and make the proper adjustments until you get it right. When you feel you have a good fit, label each piece with a marker (for instance: left inside arm, back, right outside arm, inside back) and include notes (use arrows, numbers, letters, notches, etc.) indicating what pieces to join and where to join them. Remove the basting stitches to break down the pattern into individual pieces, and trace each section onto the upholstery fabric. Cut and assemble the final slipcover.

CALCULATING FABRIC AMOUNTS

Before you make a slipcover, though, you need to know how much fabric to buy. What baffles people most is determining exactly how much yardage is required because there are so many variables involved. For instance, fabrics are sold in different widths, and then a large print may require extra yardage to allow for the repeat. Having to align stripes, plaids, or other prints in seams can also throw things off. Don't panic. If you are purchasing new fabric at a retail store there are people that can help you with this, and most stores will accept returns of a yard or more (in its original, unwashed condition, of course) with a receipt.

However, when shopping discount warehouses you are pretty much on your own and should have at least a rough estimate before you head out to make your purchase. If you are a beginner, I suggest plotting things out on graph paper.

1 Measure each section of your furniture at the widest and deepest points to determine the cutting dimensions, figuring in ½ inch for the seam allowances and 2 inches for hems.

2 Establish your working scale and roughly sketch out the shape of all the primary sections to scale on the graph paper, and label each one. (I usually count one square as one inch.)

3 On another piece of graph paper draw two parallel lines to indicate the width that your fabric will be. (Home decorating fabric generally runs about 54 inches wide. You may have to tape two or more pieces of the graph paper together to accommodate the dimensions.)

4 To make your cutting layout, cut out the labeled shapes that you sketched in step 2. Arrange the cutout pieces between the parallel lines in a configuration that uses the least amount of fabric, keeping in mind the direction of the fabric weave or pattern. For example, you want the print of the seat back to run in the same direction as the seat cushion, etc.

5 Count the number of squares along the vertical line representing the fabric to determine how many inches of fabric your cutout pieces fit into. Divide this figure by 36 to determine how many yards you will need.

note

It's always best to err on the side of surplus, so pad the number! If your fabric has a repeating motif or wide stripe or plaid that requires matching, you will definitely need extra yardage depending on the length of the repeat.

about the author

Artist and designer Sandy Stone has been breathing new life into old furnishings for nearly two decades. Her work has been featured in *Country Living* magazine and *Midwest Home*, where she was selected for the "Twin Cities 70 Best" issue in 2008. She currently works in her home studio in the Linden Hills neighborhood of Minneapolis with occasional interruptions from her husband, architect Ken Stone, her two daughters, and a grumpy West Highland Terrier. Her creations can be found at hunt & gather in Minneapolis, Minnesota (www.huntandgatherantiques.com), or viewed online at www.sandystonedesignstudio.com.

it's all on www.larkbooks.com

Got an idea for a book?
Read our book proposal guidelines and contact us.

Want to show off your work?
Browse current calls for entries.

Want to know what new and exciting books we're working on?
Sign up for our free e-newsletter.

Feeling crafty?
Find free, downloadable project directions on the site.

Interested in learning more about the authors, designers & editors who create Lark books?

acknowledgments

The opportunity to create this book was a wonderful gift for which I am truly grateful.

I want to thank Valerie Shrader, my editor (and head cheerleader) at Lark, for her thoughtful guidance and blind faith in me—and the others on the squad, especially Gavin Young, Megan Kirby, and Nancy Wood, who were instrumental in bringing it to publication.

Thanks also goes to Jane Dagmi for producing the article in Country Living *magazine that led to this collaboration.*

A special thanks to: Kristi Stratton, for her inspiration, unwavering support, and the privilege to be a part of her absolutely fabulous shop (a hurricane of creativity), hunt & gather; Kaye Monroe, for sneaking me into that shop through the back door and for her kind introduction to the "official" business; DeEtte Theisen, for her loyal friendship, constant encouragement, excellent horn blowing, and her much appreciated assistance at the shoot; and for their creative influence and constant source of raw materials, a big thanks goes to the rest of my nutty cohorts at h & g!

Thanks must also be given to Patrick Fox for his stellar photography, and to style wizard Lisa Evidon who really knows how to run a shoot! (Once again, the word hurricane comes to mind.)

For their love and support, I give warm thanks to my brothers and sisters, all six of them.

Finally and most importantly, I thank my daughters, Lydia and Norah, for "getting it" and for their patience during the making of this book, and to my husband, Ken, for so lovingly putting up with me and...well, for just about everything.

index

metric conversion chart

⅛"	3 mm	2½"	6.4 cm	11"	27.9 cm	19½"	49.5 cm	28"	71.1 cm
³⁄₁₆"	5 mm	3"	7.6 cm	11½"	29.2 cm	20"	50.8 cm	28½"	72.4 cm
¼"	6 mm	3½"	8.9 cm	12"	30.5 cm	20½"	52.0 cm	29"	73.7 cm
⁵⁄₁₆"	8 mm	4"	10.2 cm	12½"	31.8 cm	21"	53.3 cm	29½"	74.9 cm
⅜"	9.5 mm	4½"	11.4 cm	13"	33.0 cm	21½"	54.6 cm	30 "	76.2 cm
⁷⁄₁₆"	1.1 cm	5"	12.7 cm	13½"	34.3 cm	22"	55.0 cm	30½"	77.5 cm
½"	1.3 cm	5½"	14.0 cm	14"	35.6 cm	22½"	57.2 cm	31"	78.7 cm
⁹⁄₁₆"	1.4 cm	6"	15.2 cm	14½"	36.8 cm	23"	58.4 cm	31½"	80.0 cm
⅝"	1.6 cm	6½"	16.5 cm	15"	38.1 cm	23½"	59.7 cm	32"	81.3 cm
¹¹⁄₁₆"	1.7 cm	7"	17.8 cm	15½	39.4 cm	24"	61.0 cm	32½"	82.6 cm
¾"	1.9 cm	7½"	19.0 cm	16"	40.6 cm	24½"	62.2 cm	33"	83.8 cm
¹³⁄₁₆"	2.1 cm	8"	20.3 cm	16½"	41.9 cm	25"	63.5 cm	33½"	85.0 cm
⅞"	2.2 cm	8½"	21.6 cm	17"	43.2 cm	25½"	64.8 cm	34"	86.4 cm
¹⁵⁄₁₆"	2.4 cm	9¼"	22.9 cm	17½"	44.5 cm	26"	66.0 cm	34½"	87.6 cm
1"	2.5 cm	9½"	24.1 cm	18"	45.7 cm	26½"	67.3 cm	35"	88.9 cm
1½"	3.8 cm	10"	25.4 cm	18½"	47.0 cm	27"	68.6 cm	35½"	90.2 cm
2"	5.0 cm	10½"	26.7 cm	19"	48.3 cm	27½"	69.9 cm	36"	91.4 cm